AF574125

AGONY OF SURVIVAL

Agony of Survival

ALBERT A. HUTLER

with

Marvin J. Folkertsma Jr.

Glenbridge Publishing Ltd.

Library of Congress Catalog Card Number: 89-83455

International Standard Book Number 0-944435-06-8

CONTENTS

Foreword

by

Abram L. Sachar

Founding President and Chancellor Emeritus,
Brandeis University

When the long agony of the Holocaust came to an end with the liberation of the extermination camps, less than five hundred thousand Jews had survived, most of them *in extremis,* physically and psychologically. These survivors had successfully resisted Hitler's Final Solution, sustained primarily by the hope that the democratic world would help restore them to a new life in freedom and security. What they had not known was that they were to face new ordeals, compelled to survive their survival, rejected virtually everywhere, derelicts wandering between two worlds, one dead, the other apparently powerless to be born. The immigration laws of the Allied nations were structured for rigid preclusion. The sentiments of the Canadian spokesman, for instance, seemed to be subsumed in malice; referring to the admission of even selected refugees, he said grimly, "None is too many."

Such determined repudiation after the war ended was a traumatic shock for those who remained alive. Elie Wiesel, an eloquent survivor, wrote that if the victimized millions in the death camps had not clung to the dream of redemption in a free world, they would have abandoned the will to go on. Some of the Western leaders, if we are to judge them from their statements, and more from their actions, must have wished that there had been just such a failure of nerve, since they regarded the Jews as a continuing tormenting problem.

Yet the governments of the United States, Britain, and France, however grudgingly, could not cling to complete unconcern. They thus set up Displaced Persons' camps, mainly in conquered Germany and Austria. These "DP" camps provided temporary shelter and care for those who had the determination, despite the ravages of their previous experience, to undertake the hazardous treks across hostile frontiers to reach these severely limited havens.

Albert Hutler, one of the Seventh Army officials in the Stuttgart section of the American Military Government, offers a highly personalized narrative of the complex problems that clouded sympathy and understanding when the camps were first established. Policy was very much in flux as the weary survivors and harried governing staffs wrestled with complaint and irritation. There have, of course, been many such published narratives—memoirs, diaries, biographies, and histories of the period—and Hutler makes no claim to revisionist interpretations and judgments. He only supplements the well documented testimony of colleagues who served with him, hoping that his memoir will place in further perspective what the military, accused bitterly of insensitivity, had to contend with. He hoped also that the survivors, most of them emotionally unhinged by the horrors of the past, would be more patient with cumbrous legalities and the protective routine of administrative disinterest. When the governors and the governed confronted each others' frustration, Hutler's training in the area of social welfare, an experience warmed by deep compassion, made him an ideal intermediary.

Hutler's preoccupation with the canard spread by some of the military staff—that many of the Jewish survivors in the DP camps were cunningly dealing in the black market—is an example of his concern beyond bureaucratic routine. He kept reminding his critical colleagues that black marketeering was universally practiced in Germany by American officers and GIs as well as by officers and men in all the Allied armies. In the economic and social chaos of Europe in 1945, American cigarettes provided one of the few stable forms of currency, from Danzig-Gdansk to Calais. The price of a package of American cigarettes in the immediate postwar period was about twenty cents. At the Post Exchanges and Ships' Stores, however, the cost was considerably less. A PX pack of cigarettes exchanged for other goods could support an entire family for a full day. American soldiers, sailors, and merchant marines, not merely officers, regularly traded cigarettes for cameras, prewar binoculars, souvenirs, or even sexual favors.

The Jewish camp inmates followed the accepted practice of bartering their few cigarettes, often given to them by sympathetic soldiers, receiving in return fresh vegetables, milk for their children, or extra blankets to improve comfort and privacy in the barracks. Hutler asked, "Is a Jewish survivor to be blamed for imitating the practice of the GI?" Hutler's refutation, of course, was not exceptional. Nearly every Jewish chaplain, with some military officials, offered similar rebuttals. But Hutler fought irresponsible defamation up to the highest ranks, and he minced no words in demanding fairness.

Hutler was at pains also to carry a message of forbearance to his camp charges, "my Jews." He asked them to remember that the occupation authorities were overwhelmed by the complexities of governing a fragmented, defeated country, caught in the toils of one of the great migration movements of the postwar period. Even essential services were everywhere almost totally inoperative. It did not help that most of the minor officials who dealt on the operational plane with the survivors were young and inexperienced. These officials had replaced veterans of the long war and knew little about the horrors of the Holocaust, about what the survivors had endured. Often, therefore, irritation did not represent hostility; it represented tensions that were inevitable as millions of demobilized Germans returned from the battlefields. Hutler, as a conciliator, was remarkably successful. He earned the appreciation of many top officials, including General Eisenhower, and Dean Earl Harrison, President Truman's investigating deputy. In fact, when Eisenhower toured the camp in Stuttgart, accompanied by Hutler, he commented that it was the best organized DP center he had seen in Germany.

Simultaneously, Hutler savored the gratitude of spokesmen for the Jewish DP families, who never forgot what his intercession had meant to them. In the extermination hells, they had lost personal identity and had become tatooed numbers. In the American camps, they endured the anonymity of the initials, DPs. Hutler's empathy helped them regain their dignity, and this was as crucial for them as improved living conditions.

Hutler completes his memoir with vignettes of some of the men and women rehabilitated and later settled in the United States. To Hutler, these letters, also in the Epilogue, wherein sincere gratitude is not demeaned by sycophancy, give added meaning to the miracle that transformed the survivors and prepared them in spirit for participation in the creation of a sovereign Israel and for the enrichment they brought to the American scene.

ACKNOWLEDGMENTS

I frankly felt inspired to write this book largely through the influence of my mentor, colleague, and friend, Dr. Abram L. Sachar, formerly of the University of Illinois. Dr. Sachar was my history professor and later my supervisor when I became student director of the Hillel Foundation during my years in law school. A compassionate and caring man, Dr. Sachar was a role model for me and countless others who learned from him what it meant to be truly committed to helping people.

In 1984 he published a powerful book, *Redemption of the Unwanted*, that dealt with the postholocaust period of Jewish history. His work deeply affected me. When I discussed it with him, I mentioned how his account had brought back memories and had sent me rummaging through all my own records, stepping through history, reliving experiences.

When he discovered that I had kept such good records, he asked, simply, "Al, why don't you write about your time in the service, about your duties as a displaced persons officer? There hasn't been much published on this subject, and it's important that we don't forget. Why not write your own book?"

For a long moment I said nothing. Then, finally, I answered, "Why not, indeed."

To those of my family and friends who had the courage to read my manuscript through the various revisions and still thought enough of it to encourage me to continue, I express my sincerest thanks. I want to single out the efforts of my cousin Harold Goldstein, who edited an early revision; of Sandra Dijkstra, a literary agent who offered me her criticisms; of Janet Parkerson, who typed and corrected earlier revisions; of Joseph Freiberg, my Toronto friend who offered me financial help; of Ruth Gruber, whose kind words and careful review of the final drafts gave me great encouragement; and of Albert Lipson who reviewed the manuscript and made excellent suggestions for its improvement. My wife Leanore and my two daughters, Suzanne and Frankee, were a source of continuous and welcome support. They shared my feelings and philosophy about people and kept my spirits up during some hard times.

I am also deeply grateful to those who formed a part of my story: Sam Haber, a military government colleague and former executive director of the Joint Distribution Committee; Ernest Michel, a survivor who served as my receptionist and interpreter in Mannheim, recently retired from the position of executive vice-president of the New York Federation-

United Jewish Appeal; and Ethel Ostry, William Fishman, and William Colt, all senior staff members of the United Nations Rehabilitation and Relief Administration (UNRRA), who generously made available their files, scrapbooks, and other materials.

Leonard Slater, best known as the author of "The Pledge," spent hours helping me with earlier versions of the manuscript. I also wish to express my thanks to Dr. Marvin J. Folkertsma, Jr., whose writing captured the exciting experiences I had shared with the many thousands who made their journeys from hell only to encounter, after the Holocaust, the agony of survival.

Finally, I am indebted to the United States Army for giving me the opportunity to serve hundreds of thousands of people who suffered through those times of horror and hope during repatriation in Germany.

Prologue

From late March through October 1945, I served as the displaced persons officer for the region surrounding Mannheim, Germany. For eight furiously intense months my small staff and I returned nearly a quarter of a million displaced persons to their home countries. We received the homeless from all the nations of Europe, and they arrived to us in a variety of ways—off trucks, trains, planes, buses, even walking or riding bicycles or motorcycles. Pitiful creatures they were: haggard, emaciated, and hollow-eyed, still stunned by the war. Some of them were barely alive, straggling into the city on foot or wearily shuffling off a metallic, diesel-powered monster designed to haul freight or cattle. All they knew was that the war was over and a new set of authorities was in charge of their lives.

I was one of those authorities, serving in the Seventh Army American Military Government (AMG), European Civil Affairs Regiment. My unit deloused, fed and clothed them, provided shelter for overnight stays or for longer periods of time (sometimes stretching into months), and shipped them out again, usually the next day, for their homelands in Europe. Most of the homeless returned, happy to rebuild their lives. But many of them had no homes left to return to, or no country that wanted them, or they preferred death to repatriation. Those cases were the ones that made us cry, helplessly.

When I entered military service in 1942, I never anticipated that the army would give me such an excruciating job. I had no idea how my time in the military would be spent, although in retrospect I could not have asked for a more suitable assignment. In 1942 at the age of thirty-two, I was married and had one child with another on the way. I had a law degree along with several years' academic training in social welfare and a good position with a social welfare agency in Chicago. I also had an ROTC commission that had lapsed due to inactivity, and in 1941 the army simply was not interested in me. But the news from Europe during the late thirties and early forties, which carried horrible reports about Nazi persecution of the Jews, rekindled my interest in renewing my military connection. Like millions of Americans, I felt obligated to serve our country in its time of dire need.

After pestering the military bureaucracy with constant letters asking for a renewal of my commission (one of the army's responses to my entreaties suggested that my constant letterwriting was actually "impeding the war effort"!),

I finally entered military service in February 1942. In its infinite wisdom, the army sent me off to my first assignment at Camp Tyson, Paris, Tennessee, to receive training in the fine art of barrage balloon management (or something like that). I was rescued from this activity by a timely notice that a search was on for personnel qualified to serve with a new type of unit specializing in "American Civil Affairs," designated in military parlance as G5. I eagerly applied to this Military Occupational Specialty (MOS), was accepted and was transferred to Kalamazoo, Michigan, for training. From Kalamazoo I was transferred to the University of Wisconsin for instruction in German language and culture, and from there I went to Boston for shipment overseas. I arrived in England in February 1944.

After D-Day, June 6, 1944, my AMG unit followed closely on the heels of the Allied forces as the Seventh Army advanced across western Europe and into Germany in 1944 and 1945. I didn't actually begin the job for which I was trained until the spring of 1945, when the war was winding down and the Allied governments were putting their administrative apparatus for postwar Europe into place. A main focus of Allied plans was the repatriation of some seven million displaced persons throughout Europe. That was where I came in. From March through October I was in charge of repatriation for the region surrounding Mannheim, Germany, and it was during this period that the events related in the following chapters occurred.

My purpose in this book is to convey the highlights of my experiences in Germany, to capture the main themes of what happened there by relating the more noteworthy occurrences. I have not attempted to catalogue everything that happened; that would take too long and perhaps would become tedious. I have also avoided providing a statistical catalogue from that period, for such material is available from other sources. My main concern is to focus on the human element, the individuals behind the statistics, to tell of their powerful and frequently incredible tales of survival in a land ruled by the most brutal regime in history.

Naturally this task required considerable research. I reviewed letters I wrote to my wife, Leanore, during the war; I pored through old books; I examined military pamphlets, photographs, army directives, regulations, and orders, as well as other government records; and, of course, I rekindled and relived my own memories. One cannot remember everything; unpleasant events one often tries to forget. But this period made such an indelible imprint on my memory and my life, that I found I could account for and reconstruct nearly every significant occurrence of those years. Indeed, some episodes I remember as clearly as if they had happened yesterday.

Chapter One

ENTERING GERMANY

The Approach to Mannheim

During the last week of March 1945, my detachment of the Second European Civil Affairs Regiment, United States Seventh Army, moved briskly in the wake of advancing combat troops toward Ludwigshafen and Mannheim. Our journey carried us across France to the lower Rhineland along roads littered with the wreckage and debris of war. The charred ruins of Germany's most formidable machines of war—Tiger II tanks, *Jagdpanther* tank destroyers, *Flakpanzer IV "Wirbelwind"* anti-aircraft guns, eighty-eight millimeter guns, trucks, armored personnel carriers, and assorted other weapons and vehicles—laid scattered along the sides of roads or under the rubble of nearby buildings. We tossed them fitful glances and slogged onward. The twisted wreckage of Hitler's Germany, still dangerous and fearsome, loomed before us.

Bloated remains of dead horses and cows also dotted fields and roads. Their stench turned our heads, quickened our pace. Overhead, long plumes trailing behind American bombers, B-17 "Flying Fortresses," or B-24 "Liberators" etched the distant sky. Darting P-51 fighter-bombers, the magnificent aircraft that had cleared the sky of the Luftwaffe, spat angry, buzzing sounds that penetrated the bomber's familiar drone. Unassailable in the air and unstoppable on the ground, the Allied armies marched into Germany.

My unit entered Ludwigshafen on March 27 and advanced quickly to the shores of the Rhine River, which separated that town from Mannheim. Allied forces had earlier breached the Rhine farther north, near Remagen, and the American Third and Seventh armies were sweeping across the central German plain. Mannheim, however, had not been taken. The Neckar Valley, a triangular area formed by the Rhine and Neckar rivers, was still in German hands. Our assignment was to establish an American Military Government (AMG) in Mannheim as soon as it had been cleared of enemy troops. We were not sure how long that would take or how difficult the task would be.

During the evening of the twenty-seventh, my unit crouched on the banks of the river waiting for the decision to cross, wondering anxiously if the Germans would put up a stiff resistance. The night's blackness pervaded our thoughts, drowning us with gloom. We peered across the shimmering waters. A small vessel approached, its rhythmic, lapping sounds indicating that it was a rowboat. It finally beached on the shore and two men hopped out. Although the situation was not threatening, our troops quickly surrounded them as I approached with my commanding officer, Colonel Winning.

"Who are you," I demanded. Although looking haggard, they actually were dressed in suits. But their answer was in Polish, so another officer, who was fluent in that language, took over.

"Where are you from? Why did you come across the river?" he asked.

Cold, frightened, one of them said, "To escape! To get out of the city!"

"Had you been captive there?"

"No, no. We just came the day before. The city is burning."

That was true enough. We could see and smell Mannheim's destruction from a long distance, for much of the city still burned from the incendiaries dropped by Allied bombers.

"Where are the Germans?"

"Gone, leaving, getting out fast!"

We welcomed the report of the German retreat but greeted it with suspicion. The Germans were ruthless and clever in war. They had been known to send "plants" across enemy lines to spread false information, so we were wary about this piece of good news.

AMG personnel did not have the authority to decide how to act on their information, so the officer doing the questioning snapped, "Take them to the commander." They were led to the infantry officer in charge. Shortly afterward, we received orders to move across the river; apparently their credentials and story had checked out.

The infantry crossed over on a pontoon bridge constructed by the engineer corps. My unit boarded rubber rafts and rowboats. Silently, we made the crossing. Soft, random breezes gently brushed across the water; our boats pushed through the surface like blunt, slowly moving arrows, leaving rippled wakes behind us. We nervously awaited some signs of defense—rifle fire or machine guns—but none came. Landing on the other side, our AMG group proceeded to follow the infantry to the city of Mannheim.

We advanced toward the city under a full moon, which gave off a pale light, causing the drifting clouds to splash soft, irregular shadows on the ground. Following closely behind the infantry, we looked for the town museum where we were supposed to bed down for the evening. The muffled pops of random rifle fire echoed in the distance, and the sky lit up intermittently with anti-aircraft fire. The distant monotone hum of Allied bombers descended upon us—a perpetual soundtrack of war. Other than these sounds, the streets of Mannheim were hushed, a morguelike aftermath of war's desolation. Doors and windows were tightly shuttered, and none of the city's inhabitants was in evidence; either they had fled or were huddled in cellars. Their absence did nothing to calm us down. On the contrary, our nerves were jittery, our senses alert, and our eyes struggled to pierce the foreboding darkness. Everyone strained to catch any flitting, dangerous movement in the shadows as we continued to step out our tense, deliberate advance through the black streets of the city.

American and British bombers had demolished much of Mannheim. Ahead of us, sheets of flame propelled to the sky, devouring the remains of gutted buildings and homes. Although it was very dark, we could see well enough to walk around the heaps of bricks and twisted metal that littered our way. Wisps of smoke from collapsed buildings still steamed upward against the background of angry, reddish orange flashes assaulting the blackness of the night. The houses were dusted over with the grayish residue of repeated bombings. Among these ruins there remained intact an occasional lamppost or building facade. They stood alone and mute, like awkward, embarrassed sentinels, reflecting the resilience of some cultural artifacts that for unexplainable reasons had escaped the surrounding destruction.

Our progress through the ruined city was without incident, but we did have difficulty finding our way about. The deeper we penetrated into the city the darker the night became. We lost contact with the combat troops and had trouble locating the museum among the devastated buildings and streets. We continued to search for some recognizable landmarks, until we found ourselves at the outskirts of town staring at a large open pasture, palely lit by the moon's soft glow. I stared at the scene dumbly, with appreciation. No bomb craters, no smoke, no dead bodies; just a clear open field, silent and pure. Its soothing beauty caressed our weary eyes.

Unfortunately, the field was also the front line of our infantry advance, a fact that became clear to me when I was approached by an outraged major who asked us in barracks language what we were doing there.

"American Military Government," I responded, somewhat defensively.

He sneered. "The area has to be secured before you can 'govern' it, Lieutenant!"

Finding it impossible to refute such airtight logic, I simply responded, "Yessir."

"Where is your commanding officer?"

"I'll take you to him, sir. Could you follow me please?"

We approached my superior, Colonel Winning. The colonel, a tall and slender man with a sharp nose, strong chin, and a high forehead covered with thick, dark hair, had been a college professor before joining the American Military Government for duty in Germany. Although compassionate and sensitive, Winning could be direct and thoroughly military when the occasion demanded. The major saluted curtly and was respectful but succinct.

"Sir, this is a combat area. Get your men out of here and fast, before you all get killed."

Colonel Winning outranked him, of course, but was in no position to argue and it made no sense to drag things out. He tipped his head sharply and answered, "Certainly, Major." Then, looking at me, he issued a nonspoken command, "Lieutenant!"

"Right away, sir. I'll move the men back."

The major acknowledged this exchange with a quick nod and a hasty exit. As he left, I thought I heard him mutter something like, "Those idiots [or the army slang equivalent] are going to slow us up!" which seemed to be more important to him at the moment than our well-being. But I hardly wanted to take issue with his priorities. Instead, I gladly issued orders to return to Mannheim.

We finally found the museum in the heart of the city. The darkness of the night and our own exhaustion made us oblivious to its magnificent outlines and displays. Relieved and tired, we unloaded our gear and slept on the stone hardness of the museum's floors. The war continued as we slept, with sounds of shell firing, machine gun outbursts, and clanking tanks in our ears. In this unpretentious manner, American Military Government arrived in the city of Mannheim, Germany.

First Encounters

I had studied Mannheim in a rigorous training course for AMG officers at the University of Wisconsin the previous year. The instructors had taught us conversational German and had given thorough briefings on aspects of southwestern Germany, especially on the provinces of Baden and Württemberg. I thus knew that Mannheim's *Rathaus* (city hall) had been destroyed, which is why we had to look for other accommodations for our headquarters. I immediately set out upon this task with several members of my AMG staff.

The daylight exploded with stark scenes of the destruction we had stepped through the previous evening. Advancing through wrecked cities was standard fare for our troops, but the effects of American air power never ceased to shock us. Ghostly, skeletal remains of once magnificent buildings silhouetted the skyline; their windows appeared like the darkened apertures of multitudes of hollowed out, chalky gray skulls, looking not outward to the world but inward to a dead abyss. Streets were filled with heaps of rubble, occasionally punctuated by grotesquely twisted and misshapen lengths of metal that once represented lampposts, fence railings, utility pipes, and other accoutrements of modern civilization. We rumbled through the streets in our jeeps, aghast at the city's devastation and wondering if there were a single building fit for our headquarters.

We finally found one that had survived American air strikes as well as the self-destructive madness of the retreating German troops. It was a nondescript place, reflecting less the former grandeur of the shattered Reich than the stony, drab officiousness of the Nazis' ponderous and oppressive bureaucracy. Symbols of Nazism filled every corner. We promptly removed them all—pictures, emblems, flags, Nazi memorabilia of all sorts—nothing remained. Our offices were clean and Spartan, consisting only of a few chairs, desks and tables, some bookcases, and assorted administrative implements.

My unit also secured places to sleep and eat. For the officers' quarters we commandeered an apartment complex that had been hastily abandoned in Neckarstadt, a suburb of Mannheim. Like our office, it was filled with Nazi insignia and uniforms, photographs of Hitler, and books on the Third Reich, all of which we threw out. The rest of the furnishings, including silverware and china, glassware, kitchen implements, a well stocked pantry with food, wine, and liquor, and even some paintings and other art work, we saved and used. My unit created an officers' mess by taking over an entire restaurant, complete with its chef, two waitresses, a bus boy, and a dishwasher—a very convenient package deal. The enlisted men set up their own kitchen in a garage next to their apartments so they could eat their meals outdoors or in their own living quarters. We were now ready to begin our job.

It would not be easy. As the Allied armies had approached Germany, the civil government officials of the Reich had completely lost control of the population. By the time we arrived to establish a military government, Mannheim had been reduced to anarchy. The city was now a hodgepodge dumping ground of nationalities and displaced persons, including the Germans themselves, slave laborers brought in from the east, Nazi collaborators, refugees and stateless persons, prisoners of war, concentration camp survivors, and aimless wanderers of various descriptions, a quarter of a million in all, we estimated—and all frequently at odds with one another. The area was in a polyglot state of nature, raw and threatening.

At least fifteen different nationalities bustled in the three hundred-mile region of southwestern Germany, which included the cities of Mannheim, Heidelberg, Stuttgart, Darmstadt, Karlsruhe, and Heilbronn. Many of them had organized into tribal groupings in order to survive. They camped everywhere—in office buildings, warehouses, city halls, the Mannheim museum, or just in open fields. The camps were self-governed by elected leaders. All the national groups met their needs by looting, stealing, and living off the land. Survival was the first priority, no matter whose army was in the vicinity.

Looting ravaged the area; it was a practice that cut across every nationality and every social class. As we drove around the city's dusty, rubble-strewn roads, we witnessed many well-dressed Germans carrying suitcases filled with loot, while less dignified individuals in rags toted filthy rucksacks. Some national groups operated like urban gangs, fighting with one another as well as collaborating to achieve common goals, in the sacking of a warehouse, for instance. Naturally, our first priority was to stop the looting and restore order. One could not go through the city without seeing the most brazen acts of lawlessness.

A good example of Mannheim's chaotic state of affairs occurred during my second day in the city, after we had secured our headquarters building. I had left my jeep at the building and had walked a few blocks to see the commander of an infantry company when I passed a warehouse on the way. Strange sounds emitted from the structure—random shouts, shuffling feet, and boxes scrapping across the floor. I stepped around the back to an alley and peered in, unobserved.

What I saw shocked me: looters were systematically gutting the building, removing everything useful. They passed bags of food, tins, cartons, and boxes of all sizes from hand to hand and then out through broken windows to collaborators waiting outside. I had to marvel at the degree of organization displayed. Families seemed to work as teams. Oid women carried the lighter bags filled with foodstuffs, while children handed boxes to their parents who in turn handed them to others to carry away; a teamlike "bucket brigade" efficiency governed their actions. Bringing this operation to a halt was clearly beyond the scope of a single American officer, so I quietly dashed away and returned about an hour later with some military police. Together we made a dramatic entrance.

"Halt!" I shouted—an order that means the same in German and English.

The sight of an American officer accompanied by military police with weapons drawn gave them all a shock, and pandemonium broke loose. People scattered off in all directions, bumping, shoving, and scrambling their way to the nearest exits. Many with their arms full dropped everything and frantically tried to scurry out of the building, pushing aside those who got in their way. Others, with no ready means of escape, just stood there, frozen.

My whole point, of course, was to get them to leave, but in a more quiet and orderly fashion. I had many other things to do and policing warehouses was not one of them. But I had obviously not gone about this task in the right way, and I became concerned that someone would get injured or that more goods would be damaged unless things settled down. Eventually, we were able to bring the situation under control by repeating the order for them to stop, which I continued to bark out like a First Lieutenant of the Wehrmacht. I figured at least they were probably used to that.

"Halt!" I repeated. "Bleiben Sie auf der Stelle stehen! Bewegen Sie sich nicht. Wir tun Ihnen nichts! (Stop! Stay where you are! You won't get hurt, but don't move!)"

Those who remained finally calmed down. They faced us with looks of fear and anxiety, wondering how these new authorities would treat them.

"Jawohl," one of them said.

I tried to question them, but to little avail. Interestingly, like children caught in the act of stealing or engaging in some mischief, no one admitted to knowing anything, including who they were or where they were from. We heard numerous cries of innocence and endless "Ich weiss nichts (I don't knows)," but few admissions of guilt. This came as no surprise. In a situation where the first rule of behavior is staying alive, who can say what is right and what is wrong? They were hungry and needed to eat; we knew that. Indeed, it was our job to feed and care for them, but naturally they weren't aware of our mission and had no reason to trust us. My basic concern at that moment was simply to clear them out and safeguard the warehouse.

"Sie können jetzt gehen (You may go)," I said, hoping to convey a less threatening manner. Taking the thought one step further, I tried to inform our hapless scavengers that they could keep what they had in their possession, but that they had to leave and could not return. "Behalten Sie Ihre Sachen (You may keep what you have)," I said.

Stares of disbelief greeted that message. Several people asked the question, "Sind wir festgenommen? (Are we under arrest?)"

"Nein," I replied evenly, "sie sind keine Gefangene (No, you are not under arrest)."

Hardly! I exclaimed to myself. What would I do on my second day in Mannheim with a bunch of half-starved, miscreant civilians, whose motivation to sack a building filled with foodstuffs was more compelling than my official inclination to kick them out?

"I just want you to get the hell out of here! Ok?" I blurted out in frustration, letting my thoughts slip out of my mouth in English. The tone seemed right, but of course the language was wrong. Back to the German: "Sie können nehmen was Sie haben. Aber hier sind Sie nicht erlaubt. (You may take what you have. But you're not allowed here.)"

Better, I thought. All they had to do was to leave quietly with what they had. Obviously, bursting in like the cavalry in a movie Western had failed to accomplish my purpose, so I figured a softer pitch with an agreeable message would do the trick.

It didn't. Again, uncomprehending looks were exchanged.

I knew they had understood what I had said; they just didn't believe I would let them go without incident. My approach so far had been futile, and I was losing patience. I wanted to get out of there myself.

Time to try the tough act again. Thus, embellishing a ferocious scowl with my most forceful, threatening German, I bellowed, "Es ist verboten! Gehen Sie! Hauen Sie ab! Kommen Sie nicht wieder zurück! Fort von hier! (This is forbidden! Now go! Get out! Don't come back! Leave the premises!)"

This combination worked. Finally, convinced it was safe to leave without incident, they dashed out of the warehouse with as much as they could carry, ran out onto the streets, and disappeared into the ruins of the city without so much as a departing "danke." The warehouse was somewhat less well stocked, of course, but no one had gotten hurt. I sent off a report to the military government food office about the incident. The officials later took action to secure the warehouses against looters, and the case was closed, for the moment, at least. The MPs returned, and I went back to headquarters to get my jeep.

I soon discovered, however, that securing warehouses was the least of our problems during the first days of our occupation.

Asserting Allied Authority

Initial encounters between American troops and German citizens were stiff, proper, and cautious. When the Germans first saw us, they were impressed, as they should have been. When we marched through Mannheim to take over our headquarters building, the American soldiers presented a fine picture of military decorum. With clean-shaven faces, proper uniforms festooned with as many ribbons as one's military accomplishments warranted, sparkling, shined boots, and sidearms boldly hanging from the hips, we displayed American military élan with pride and zeal. The citizens reacted with a mixture of fear and propriety. Men stood at attention, tipped their hats, bowed their heads, and occasionally clicked their heels with the deference a subordinate customarily renders to his superior. Women stepped off the sidewalks looking downward and away when GIs approached. Children gave us wide-eyed, sometimes fawning obedience.

It didn't last long, though. Throughout the war, American soldiers demonstrated their capacity for great discipline and bravery under pressure, but their fundamentally civilian outlook on life usually overwhelmed the temporary military bearing imposed upon them by the army when that pressure was removed. Thus, when the military threat receded, many of our soldiers in Mannheim reverted to some very sloppy, nonmilitary behavior, which, we quickly learned, impeded our efforts to accomplish our mission.

Only a few days after occupation, Germans who came to my office saw the bodies of headquarters guards splayed carelessly over benches outside the building. Many casually smoked cigarettes or cigars during duty hours and wore rumpled uniforms with open shirts and no ties, unpressed trousers, and scuffed-up boots. Saluting became rare and awkward, indicating their lack of seriousness about our presence and mission; in short, they appeared "soft" and slipshod. They certainly didn't seem bent on becoming Germany's new masters, which the Germans initially supposed was their purpose. They just didn't look the part.

Often they didn't act the part, either. A familiar spectacle splashed across the villages and cities of occupied Germany: a scrubby-faced GI with his helmet cocked rakishly above his forehead, smilingly passing out Hershey bars, Wrigley gum, C and K rations, and home-baked goods sent from overseas. Americans had especially open hearts for children with gaunt bodies, outstretched hands, and pitifully begging eyes; they were "easy marks." But Germans looked upon this behavior with disdain and contempt, wondering just what sort of conqueror had taken over their country. For years they had rendered unquestioning obedience to their superiors—particularly to military authorities—which often verged on the slavish. It was hard for them to believe that American soldiers represented the wave of their country's future.

Within a week of our occupation, we were having problems with the population. Many Germans became arrogant toward and contemptuous of the occupation troops, mistaking Americans' frequently carefree attitudes for weakness and lack of resolve. I saw instances on the streets where pushy Germans insolently elbowed their way through American soldiers who got in their way. Others discovered that they could talk back to American authorities with impunity, or even refuse to carry out our orders. Their facial expressions outraged me: icy, narrowed eyes issuing looks of superciliousness and rancor, sneering lips, and muffled remarks under their breaths that they probably thought I didn't hear or couldn't understand. American officers could not tolerate such behavior. Something had to be done.

And it was. After a hastily convened officers' meeting, Colonel Winning issued orders that required American soldiers to clean up their act and the German population to respect our authority. The GIs were required to adhere strictly to the dress code by wearing the full uniform, which consisted of blouse and tie, shined shoes, and prominently displayed military decorations. Smoking and lounging during duty hours were strictly forbidden, even while walking the streets of the city. Fraternization with the enemy was also not allowed—we were still at war, after all—and officers were always to be saluted. In short, soldiers were required to maintain a proper military bearing at all times while carrying out their tasks in the occupation and administration of Germany.

We also warned the Germans that the American Military Government would brook no nonsense in its dealings with them. Any form of disrespect toward American soldiers or disobedience to the occupation authorities would result in arrest, incarceration, and trial before an American military court. We demanded their respect, and we got it. Indeed, when the directives were sent out, visions of the Frank Capra "Why We Fight" films, which were required viewing for all military personnel, were refreshed in our memories, reminding us who they were, who we were, and what our task was.

The short-term effects of the rules were considerable. The population didn't like us any better, but we weren't there on a goodwill mission. We were there to administer the area and, bluntly speaking, to ship people back to where they belonged, if possible. However, continuing to deal with the Germans as enemies, or even former enemies, became increasingly difficult as the year progressed, as we shall see.

Our Displaced Persons Section: A Routine Day

A routine day about the offices of the American Military Government in the months following our entry into Mannheim is difficult to describe, because no two days were ever alike. We were continually confronted with experiences that astonished us; events that at first struck us as extraordinary later became routine.

Even minor matters caused alarm, and sometimes wry amusement. For instance, when I first affixed my name, title, and responsibilities on my office door—Lieutenant Albert A. Hutler, Section Chief, Displaced Persons and Public Welfare

Section, American Military Government—people stopped and stared at it for a while, their faces expressing a mixture of curiosity, fear, and incomprehension. I couldn't understand this reaction until someone explained to me the uncanny resemblance between my name and that of the former dictator of the Third Reich. I was told that if an umlaut (¨) were placed above the "u" in Hutler, the German pronunciation of my name would be very similar to that of "Hitler." This bizarre incongruity was lost on no one and initially was the subject of some grim, although perhaps misplaced, humor. That a man with the name of A. Hutler (or Hütler) should be put in charge of salvaging the lives of those who had survived the death camps and labor brigades of A. Hitler was an astounding coincidence, a gratuitous irony.

But the months that followed were filled with coincidences, ironies, and occasional shocks. We found ourselves commandeering office buildings, apartment complexes, houses, restaurants, and at least one castle. We constructed medical facilities, kitchens, recreation fields, schools, and places of worship. We sponsored church services, aided newspapers, wrote reports, read memos, occasionally defied higher officers, sent people to jail, and requisitioned, for the use of our displaced persons (DPs), every kind of thing ever found in a house. We cradled babies while helping their mothers board trains to their homelands, hoping they would endure the stuffy, clanking, and grinding rigors of a five hundred-mile railway journey. We helped those who wanted to go home after the war as well as those who did not, and we tried to counsel those who could not believe that the war was actually over.

Much of the time we listened to people, discussed our alternatives, and ordered things done. Sometimes we even wept; other times we were too stunned and tired to weep or to react at all. We listened to impassioned stories in a dozen or so languages from individuals who pleaded with us to move them east, west, north, or south, or not to move them at all. I listened to accounts from Germans who said they knew nothing of the Holocaust and from Jews who begged us to protect them from the hatred of those very same Germans. I marveled at how many of our soldiers showed more compassion, respect, and understanding for the defeated enemy than they did for the Germans' helpless victims. One moment I sat speechless pondering the nature of a people capable of tending flower gardens as well as building crematoria only to face, the next moment, the arrogance of a heel-clicking Prussian who insisted that the Americans should join what was left of the German army to fight the Russians.

In short, I was often astonished by what was going on around us, by the requirements of my duties and those of my staff, and by the obstacles in our way. Unusual, sometimes traumatic events pervaded our lives, our work. Surprises became common; the extraordinary, part of our routine.

Chapter Two

LIFE AT THE OFFICE

Of *Gauleiters* and DPs

Much of my daily routine was actually spent away from the office, handling matters that eventually ended up on my desk as paperwork to plow through and act upon. Everything we did had to be justified, written about, double-checked, and sometimes debriefed. One such case involved my occasional assistance of a couple of sergeants from the Public Safety Section of the AMG, which was also located in our headquarters building. Although I didn't like this duty very much, the professionalism of the two men impressed me. I sat next to one of them, observing, while the other went about his job probing the past of an individual suspected of having engaged in Nazi activities during or prior to the war years. The questioner was good.

The sergeant's stern visage penetrated the German's defenses, causing him to move his sweating, quivering head down and to the side, muttering nervously, "Ich weiss nicht." The slouched figure drooped his torso lower and covered the back of his head with both hands, rubbing his neck. His body, rotund and squat, was hunched over with his elbows planted on his knees. The short wooden chair creaked as he shifted.

The sergeant's companion got up, stepped forward with ominous deliberation, and took over the questioning.

"You were a *Gauleiter* [a minor Nazi city official], were you not?" This was translated.

"Jawohl."

"And what were your responsibilities?"

"The same as all Gauleiters, to carry out party orders."

"We have evidence that you were involved in *Kristallnacht* in 1938 and in the Gestapo raids to round up Jewish citizens, which took place during the following year and especially in 1944. Is that true?"

Kristallnacht, literally, crystal night, was the name given to that infamous night when rampaging Nazis destroyed property, razed synagogues, and smashed shops owned by Jews throughout Germany during the evenings of November 9–10, 1938. The event was so named because of the huge amount of glass that was broken and littered on the streets of every major German city. The *Kristallnacht* question was a new slant, and I was interested to hear what answer he would give.

"I know nothing of such things. I was aware of *Kristallnacht*. That is all."

Preposterous, I thought. You were probably out there heaving rocks through windows with the rest of the hoodlums.

We had been there for five hours with this fellow. The sergeant doing the questioning looked at me as if to say he felt this was four hours too many.

His temper rising, he placed his big hands on the slumping figure's shoulders and snapped his body backward. The violent jerk sprayed droplets of sweat from the German's head to the floor around him.

"We have proof, Kraut! Do you *verstehen* that? Proof! Like eyewitnesses to everything written down here." He waved a sheath of official-looking papers in the Gauleiter's face. "Now, are you going to play games with me all night, or..."

"Hold it." His companion restrained him, flitting a glance in my direction. We despised Nazis, but Americans did not mimic their methods, no matter how impatient or outraged we became. The questioner relaxed his grip. "We're getting nowhere, and I'm tired. Let's wrap it up now and continue tomorrow. OK?"

Releasing his hold on the German's shoulders, the other sergeant sighed in disgust. "All right, then. Tomorrow."

"I've got to leave now," I said. "There's a train of DPs coming in the morning sometime, and I've got to swing by a few camps before then."

"OK, Lieutenant."

I left for the officers' quarters. Shortly afterward, the two American sergeants also departed, expecting to continue their familiar duty of tracking down and questioning former Nazi officials in the Mannheim area on the following day.

At 0300 hours—three o'clock in the morning—I stood at the Mannheim railroad station supervising the disposition of a fresh trainload of DPs sent into the city by Seventh Army Headquarters. My personal jeep always stayed ready at our office building so I could speed off at a moment's notice to meet the trains and make sure that all the DPs were taken care of properly. Fortunately, my excellent staff made it less necessary for me to be everywhere all of the time.

Harold Weiss, a sergeant in my unit who served as an interpreter, was with me. He was an American Jew who traced his background to Hungary; his parents had emigrated before the war. Weiss was a striking figure, short in stature but with darkly handsome features, accented by a crisply meticulous appearance, a naturally ebullient, good-natured temperament, and an absolutely first-rate intellect. In fact, in my view he was a linguistic genius. Weiss was able to absorb the essentials of a new language within a matter of weeks, enabling him to interpret and translate with the aplomb and professionalism of a native. Given the multiplicity of nationalities we had to cope with on a daily basis, he was, to say the least, a very handy guy to have around.

Sergeant Andrew Sikora was also on duty. He was a tall, blond young fellow fluent in Polish and extraordinarily adept at organizing the movements of the DPs from the camps to the railroad stations. Weiss was in charge of railway and truck departures from Mannheim, so the work of these two sergeants complemented each other.

We were routinely assisted by some two hundred enlisted men from nearby American units. We also used numerous DPs fluent in the languages we needed, given the nationality of the incoming passengers. Usually these DPs were waiting to return to Eastern European countries and remained with us because their repatriation had been delayed for some reason. The GIs volunteered their services; the DPs did also, but were paid in German military marks. We needed all the help we could get.

I looked at my watch. It was 0330 hours—3:30 A.M. My staff and I had been up for about thirty-five hours—or was it forty? Forty-five? I had forgotten. I peered across the distant tracks through red-rimmed, bleary eyes. So much activity was being crammed into each twenty-four-hour period that night and day had merged into one another, distinguished only by the amount of light we had to work in. Finally, the train became faintly visible as it emerged out of the night's dark background. The locomotive, a black, massive bulk, hissed and squealed as it pulled into the depot; a long procession of cars clanked and rattled behind it, breaking the silence of the night. I breathed deeply and tried to prepare myself to endure another round of our intense, systematic routine.

The rhythmic huff and hiss of the train's engines slowed as it came to a stop, culminating in a long, whistling discharge of steam. Heads and arms protruding from windows of the coaches enlivened the metallic impersonality of the cars that trailed behind. The travelers were weary, we knew; exhaustion suppressed their joy. The trip to Mannheim was only one step of their journeys homeward. We would have them for twenty-four hours, and then send them off again. In a few days, they would be in France, Belgium, or Holland;

a few thousand would be in Italy; many more would be fighting for their survival under a new occupation regime in some Eastern European country. And the next day we would be going through the same motions with tens of thousands of others just like them.

The process for transporting repatriates by truck was similar. In fact, before the Nazi surrender, we had worked out an arrangement with the transportation section of the Seventh Army to use their supply vehicles to carry DPs back to points west in Holland, Belgium, Luxembourg, or France. Each week, fifty to one hundred ten-ton trucks passed through the Mannheim region carrying supplies to the front. They used the same route for their return trip. The transportation section agreed to load their empty trucks with DPs, after we provided the returnees with the necessary food, clothing, and medical supplies always kept handy at a portable building constructed by the Engineers. We moved thousands of people that way—five, sometimes six or eight, thousand over a twenty-four-hour period—using twenty- or thirty-truck convoys. This arrangement was an excellent example of cooperation among various parts of the vast army bureaucracy, indicating that repatriation was a high priority for the army, even before the end of the war.

I looked at the passengers as they slowly, sometimes painfully, stepped onto the depot platform, stretching their limbs, rubbing their eyes, quickly assessing their surroundings. The cars contained individuals of every age and description: old and young, some dead (unable to survive the journey), and even some about to be born. Many were starving; almost all were weak and haggard. Some were dressed in striped prisoners' uniforms, and others were hardly dressed at all. A few were even well-dressed, carrying expensive luggage and toting well-wrapped boxes. The sight of such persons always perturbed me and made me speculate about their origins. Most of the concentration camp survivors, of course, came in far worse shape.

There were other, worse shocks. Women assisted off the train by sympathetic GIs startled their helpers by revealing charcoal black, tattooed numbers on their arms. Children too weak to move were carried by parents and soldiers, the latter often unable to suppress a wayward tear trickling down a cheek. Many American troops, freshly arrived for occupation duties, had never seen youngsters in such condition. None of the children—in fact, not many of the adults—had ever witnessed soldiers assist the homeless like this.

For a brief moment, before some distraction carried my thoughts away, I stood there and watched.

You never get used to it, I thought. It may become routine, but you never get used to it. If you do, you're no longer a human being.

"Don't you know how to carry a baby, for crying out loud?"

I turned my head in the direction of the voice. Individuals were piling out of the cars now, their arms filled with their possessions, sometimes with babies wrapped in ragged clothing.

"I'm sorry, Sergeant," a young GI said sheepishly, awkwardly cradling an infant while several DPs standing by him handled their luggage. "I don't have much experience with this."

"Well, get some."

"I plan to."

I smiled. My staff had everything under control.

The trains coming in from Ludwigshafen were forty cars long, thirty-nine individuals to a car. When they arrived in Mannheim our trucks were waiting to carry the DPs to our camps. A forty-car train required twenty-five trucks. After the DPs arrived in one of our camps, they were registered, given food and a brief medical examination, deloused, and bedded down. Children went to our nursery where we provided care for about five hundred individuals a day, many of whom were malnourished. We gave them milk, cereal, macaroni, biscuits, cake, and chocolate. Feeding the adults became a massive project, requiring the establishment of a soup kitchen. Sometimes we fed as many as eleven thousand people a day. Our unit also administered a dormitory for unattached children under the age of sixteen. In short, we were equipped to attend to all the needs that could reasonably be addressed in a twenty-four-hour period for people that spanned such ranges of age, health, and background.

Occasionally, we were in a position to add a special touch. When the first French DPs were scheduled to leave Mannheim for France, I suggested over lunch with a French officer that each railway car be supplied with a keg of wine.

"Brilliant, mon ami!" came the response.

"It sounds good to me," I said, agreeing entirely with his conclusion. "We could supply the wine, but it would be furnished by French officers as a welcome home gift. Great for the morale, don't you think?" Of course, a keg of wine is great for anyone's morale, I thought, but especially for the French.

"We can put it on the cars at Ludwigshafen, at the train depot. They can have it on the way home."

"And I'll promise to keep things quiet so it remains your surprise."

And that, we all thought, was an inspired idea, something to add spice to the tedium and discomfort of railway trips home.

Initially the arrangement worked well. Sergeant Weiss, who prepared the report on their departures, said that the return of the first French DPs was a grand *fête champêtre*. They kissed the ground of their homeland, danced in the streets, and, characteristically, saturated themselves and their loved ones with wine and song. Families and French officials greeted them with praise, breath-squeezing embraces, endless rounds of toasts, and celebrations.

There is a nasty side to this story, however. When the French government announced that the returnees would be given small grants to help them restore their lives, vehement and bitter protests erupted throughout the country, much of it directed against repatriated French Jews by other Frenchmen. I had helped a lot of those Frenchmen, now frothing with bigotry and hatred, return to France. "Down with the Jews!" screamed the marching hordes on the streets of Paris, I was told. "Hitler should have killed all of them!" When word of the demonstrations trickled back to us in Mannheim, the wine shipments on French railway cars from the American sector stopped immediately. Sometimes good ideas end up that way.

"Lieutenant Hutler?"

"Yes."

"There's a message for you."

A corporal handed me a wrinkled paper with a brief note scrawled on it. I read it and stuffed it into my pocket.

"Tell him I can't come now."

"It sounded important, sir."

There was some commotion near the rear of the train. I looked in that direction, turned my head this way and that, but couldn't make it out.

"It sounded important," he repeated.

"Yeah," I peered over his shoulder, straining to see what was going on. Confound it. If only I were taller. "Look, I'm busy here. Are you going back to headquarters?"

"Yes sir."

"Good. I'll be there after we get this group to camp."

"Yes sir."

Quickly, I walked across the station deck, carefully pushing my way through people, and tried to step closer to the cause of the ruckus. But clumps of individuals got in my way and I still couldn't see much. Those around me didn't pay any attention to my rank.

"Hold it! Careful! Easy as it goes. Got it?"

"Yeah, I got it. Watch that railing."

"Right."

Several soldiers struggled to fit a stretcher through the awkward, constricting doorway passage of a railway car. I could see the carrier shift awkwardly with the movements of its cargo, a writhing figure under heavy blankets. High-pitched moans stood out among the hubbub of shuffling people and scraping luggage. They freed the stretcher from the stuffy confines of the railway coach and hurried it to an ambulance that was parked nearby. Two medics quickly loaded the stretcher aboard. The vehicle raced off to the hospital.

"Will he be all right?" I asked one of the helpers who had just turned his charge over to the medics.

"It's a she, sir, and I think so, if they get her to the hospital in time."

"In time for what?"

He looked at me as though I were an idiot. "To have her baby, sir."

"Oh, yeah, right, OK. Well, then, good work."

"Thank you, sir."

Maybe I was an idiot. No, I consoled myself, I was just tired. I looked at my watch again; it was now five o'clock in the morning. In another hour another crew would be at Kaiser Wilhelm Kaserne and one of the apartment buildings nearby to wake up the DPs residing there, organize them into groups, put them on trucks, and take them to another station. At 0800 hours our troops would board the DPs on freight cars or coaches, provide them with twelve hours' rations, and ship them out to different camps, from which they would then be shipped home. A second train would be ready for boarding at 1330 hours—1:30 P.M.—with another group of DPs, this time headed for points east. The process was endless.

I remember writing my wife the night before that supervising all this was a good life if you could keep your head and get enough sleep. My unit managed to do one but not the other; we were always short on sleep.

Since the detraining and loading of the DPs was well in hand, I decided to go back to my office, grab a bite to eat, and go through some paperwork before the round of departures began for that day.

I pulled the crumpled note out of my pocket. Better take care of that too, I thought.

Mengele, Calligraphy, and a Few Pieces of Bread

I returned to our headquarters building in a walking sleep and bumped into Captain Abraham Hasselkorn, my face brushing his branch insignia: the Star of David over two tablets of the Ten Commandments—the symbol of a Jewish chaplain.

"Good morning, Al," he said.

"Huh-yeah."

He deserved a better greeting than that. A generous man with a round face and an earnest, sincere deportment, Hasselkorn was a reform rabbi from Salinas, California. He had spent just as many seventy-two-hour days ministering to the needs of the many peoples of Europe under our temporary care as the rest of us—more, probably. He was a dear friend and a deeply compassionate person. I was just too tired to be civil.

I went into my office and sat down. Stacks of DP reports and logs of our activities cluttered my desk, staring at me—demanding, uncaring, indifferent to my state of mind. I began to page through them, looking for a recent report pertaining to today's shipment:

50 ten-ton trucks arriving at Mannheim, 2000 people

Shipped out 1000 Dutch from Ulm

Shipped out 1400 Dutch men to Maastricht, Holland, by freight car; loading at 0600 hours; rations for three-day trip

[Note to myself]: call Speyer [the French commander] re: taking Dutch women, children; we will ship French women, children by coach

1500 Italians shipped out

Move 150 beds to Bensheim camp, prepare for shipment of Russians

10 coaches to Saargumines for French women and children; add the Belgians if room permits. Coaches laid on 1700, ready for departure 1000; Rations: 80 Red Cross parcels, milk for children and expectant mothers

30 freight cars for French and Belgian men only—750 men

[Note to myself]: Begin dusting Italians; talk to Italian commander

[Note to myself]: Check QM [Quartermaster] for new dusting equipment

[Note to myself]: Talk to French commander about use of freight cars for shipping women, children. This is contrary to our policy

Talked to Colonel Steele, Major Chapin re: DP problem in their area; went to Hochenheim, found building for 800 Poles; 27 large rooms for 15 double deck beds, 10 showers, 34 toilets, kitchen in good shape

Talked to Russians about looting; they advise arrest, detention of those guilty

Moved beds from Weinheim camp to Bensheim camp

Death by accident reported—a Frenchman died of fumes escaping gas stove

Chaplain Hasselkorn met with 20 Jewish DPs with false IDs

Issued passes for them to attend his services
1200 Yugoslavs from a Lieutenant Johnstone of Mossbach
Complaints: Germans complain of DPs looting, stealing, fighting; Russian DPs complain about Germans; Jewish claims about discrimination from ration board [Note to myself: check it out]
Sentenced man one year for showing open disrespect for AMG rules

This last note brought a smile to my face, although I wasn't sure what it was doing in this stack of reports. It pertained to a well-dressed elderly man caught throwing a package over the wire fence of a German Prisoner of War camp, in spite of postings—"Do not Stop!"; "Crime to Stop!"; "Do not throw anything over the fence!"—all over the area. Because of my legal education, I sat as a judge when his case came up. The testimony revealed that the package contained a pipe and tin of tobacco for his son. But it could have been a pistol or some other weapon, so I gave him the maximum sentence of one year and a day for open defiance of AMG regulations. Apparently, Seventh Army felt the punishment was a bit stiff; they never assigned me to sit as a judge again. Perhaps they concluded that an American of Jewish faith could not be impartial in such matters. They were probably right.

I kept reading, until I confronted this message:

[Note to myself]: Average number DPs repatriated by our unit: 30,000 per month. Numbers repatriated so far, April to June: 125,000 (thereabouts)

One hundred and twenty-five thousand souls, I thought. There's still at least that many out there in the Seventh Army district waiting to be moved, and they keep coming in by the trainloads, thousands at a time.

I rubbed my eyes and cradled my head in my hands, resting my elbows on the desk. A dozing, half-conscious state engulfed me, interrupted only by a sprinkling of words in German and English, random sounds that pricked the monotone numbness of my body like tiny, wayward darts.

"*Was ist das?*… I'm sorry? … *Was ist das?* … What is this? It's the insignia for a Chaplain. I'm Jewish … *Was! Wie bitte?* … Yes, a Jewish chaplain. Pardon me, but do you speak English? Um, *Sprechen Sie Englisch?* … *Nein, Etwas* … A little bit, you say. Well, may I help you? My name is Hasselkorn, Chaplain Hasselkorn. Who are you? *Uh, Wie heissen Sie?* … Michel. Ernest Wolfgang Michel … I see. Really? … You mean, here in Mannheim? … I see … The Displaced Persons' Section? Yes, this office right here. Why don't you come with me."

Finally, "Lieutenant Hutler."

"Eh?" My head popped up with a start.

"There's someone here I think you should see."

Then, in German, "I'm Ernest Michel, sir. They told me I should come to see you, to find out what I should do."

Before me stood a gaunt young man with an earnest face, prematurely worn, attired in clean but ragged clothes. He had sandy brown hair, a high forehead, and eyes that sparkled with the vivacity of a quick intellect. He stood before me tall and thin, but not emaciated, evincing a ruggedness that overcame the slightness of his frame.

"Did I overhear you correctly? You're from . . ."

"I'm from Mannheim. My family has lived here for three hundred years, until the Nazis came and took them and me away. Now I've come back, and they told me to come here."

"You've come back. You've come back from what?"

"From concentration camps. I escaped from the last one, and finally made it to Mannheim last night. They put me in jail and told me to come here to find out what I should do."

"Wait a minute. Concentration camps? You've been to several?"

"Yes sir. The last one was Berga. We were marching off to another camp when I got away with a couple of friends. We escaped."

"Had you been in Berga a long time?"

"No, no. Before that I was in Buchenwald."

Hasselkorn cut in. "Buchenwald?"

"Yeah."

"Then had you been there, uh, these last years?" I asked.

"No, before that I was at Auschwitz."

Hasselkorn and I reacted with silence. Finally, *"Auschwitz?"*

"Yes sir, Auschwitz. I've been at eleven camps in the last five and a half years. Labor camps, slave camps, concentration camps, places like that."

Hasselkorn and I exchanged looks. He then directed a smile of appreciation to this survivor, this returnee from hell. Repeating his answers to our questions was awkward, and he did not seem to understand our astonishment. I wanted to learn more about him.

"You'll have to excuse us, Mr. Michel," I said. "We've seen a lot of people coming back from horrible places. Normally we seen them in groups. But the captain and I haven't talked with anyone who made it back from Auschwitz, not with anyone who's gotten away from it, who survived."

Michel was about to say something, but Hasselkorn broke in, "The lieutenant is in charge of the Displaced Persons' Section, but he also assists in other matters, particularly with Jewish . . . survivors."

I could not overcome the sense of awe I felt in the presence of this young man. "Mr. Michel, how did you get out of Auschwitz?" I asked.

It was a foolish, callous question. He had just come back, and now an American lieutenant was asking him to return, by way of his memory. A brief silence followed.

"Well, I was going to say that I didn't get away from Auschwitz, if by that you mean escape. I was shipped out of there; or, rather we marched out and then were shipped. I did escape with two friends, but this was during the march from Berga to some place we didn't know. And then we were lucky. There were no dogs, and the Germans didn't chase us like they probably would have a few years earlier. It was near the end of the war."

"I see. But the fact that you made it out of Auschwitz ..."

"Yeah, a couple of things saved me," he said.

We waited for him to continue.

"The first was a turn of the thumb, I guess," he said.

"What?"

"A turn of the thumb. We arrived in Auschwitz—this was the winter of forty-two to forty-three—in cattle cars, everyone packed together, men, women, children, after a seven- or eight-day trip. We lived in a cattle car for a week. We got there in the middle of the night, around two or three o'clock in the morning, I think. It was horribly cold. We were stiff and could hardly walk. But they beat us out of the cars, and then things happened so fast that you really didn't realize what was going on.

"At the railroad station there were a bunch of SS men, and they separated the men from the women—men on this side, women on that side. Everybody got separated from their families, fathers, sons, mothers, daughters, all sent to separate places. I was taken with the men in a long line down a narrow road. At the end of the road was this SS man dressed in a shiny leather jacket and white gloves. It was Dr. Mengele. After we learned more about him, we called him the Angel of Death."

"Why?"

"He did all sorts of experiments on people at the camp hospital. We never heard from them again."

I decided not to pursue this topic, not at the moment at least. "I see."

"Anyway, he's standing there and he looks at you. If his thumb turns up, you live; if it goes down, you die. You either lived or died, depending upon how he moved his thumb. If you looked healthy enough for them to get some work out of you, you lived—a little longer, at least. But sometimes they didn't need any workers, so it didn't matter if you were healthy. Then people went from cattle cars to trucks to the gas chamber. I guess they needed workers when I came, so it was thumbs up for me. That's how I made it. I didn't know that at the time, we figured it out later. I still could have gotten killed, though. Eventually, most people were killed. They told us that."

"They told you that—that you were going to be killed?"

"Well, they said that this was, you know, the end of the line. No one leaves from Auschwitz."

"But you did."

"I did. I was one of the lucky ones. But you never know what's going to happen to you, or when, from the moment you come to the moment you die. You just follow directions."

Hasselkorn and I had seen the results of the concentration camps, of course. But at that time we did not know much about the process, what the Germans did to people before they killed them or the camps were liberated. I did not know if I wanted to hear the details, but Michel's story held us fast.

"What happened then?" Hasselkorn asked.

"They put us through lines, and we took off our clothes, put them in piles, shoes here, other clothes there; it was very organized. They let us keep our glasses. Then they tattooed our arms. The guy who did mine must have been a butcher or something; my arm swelled up to double its size. That's all we had: glasses and tattooed arms, but no clothes. Then they cut off all of our hair, deloused us, and gave us striped clothes.

"After that we were assigned to blocks. I found out later that there were different camps at Auschwitz and that they had different purposes. Auschwitz Birkenau is where they had the gas chambers. Anyone going to Birkenau went up the chimney. And you smelled them. It was part of our daily lives. You knew it was going to happen to you sooner or later."

Up the chimney.

A drop of moisture softly plopped on the back of my hand; its gentle, tickling warmth traced a slow path across my skin and down to the desk top. It stirred no thought. Michel's face blurred, and I hurriedly brushed my sleeve across my eyes, cleared my throat, and said, weakly, "Go on."

"So I worked in the camp, until we were moved, until the Russians came closer to Germany and they moved us out."

"What did you do?"

"We worked at building a rubber plant. We never made any rubber, though; we just worked at building a factory. I stayed in the barracks with four or five hundred male prisoners. We got up in the morning, got coffee and a piece of bread, and then marched off to work."

"Did you ever think of escaping?"

Michel's mouth widened with a fleeting, minute expression that could not be called a smile.

"Escape? There were SS men standing there all the time, three fences, one of them electrically wired, guard towers with machine guns, dogs patrolling—you couldn't escape. It was impossible. Sometimes people ran up to the electrical fence to kill themselves, but you couldn't escape."

"But you still got out. How?"

"I was lucky. You see, everyone does hard labor, moving heavy beams, carrying sacks of cement and stuff, and we had so little to eat that people died all the time. But if a thousand died, another thousand came in to replace them. It was endless. Sometimes after just a few days of work a person was finished. He would drop, and the SS would carry him off to be gassed. Even before work began, the SS looked at you in the morning, and if you looked weak, they'd put you in trucks. When the trucks were full, off to the gas chambers.

"Others lasted longer, like me. Still, you can only work for so long, and after about four or five months, I knew I had reached the end of my strength. Then I got sick. After one of the guards beat me, I got a large wound, which developed a lot of pus. I had a horrible fever and could barely walk, but I didn't want to go to the camp hospital."

"Why not?"

"Because people who stayed at the camp hospital overnight ended up in the gas chamber. But I just couldn't stand it any more, and someone suggested that if I went there to get the wound lanced, maybe I could come back the same day, without staying overnight. That's finally what I did."

"So you didn't stay overnight."

"Actually, I did, for three or four nights, in fact."

"Then how, uh, why did they let you . . ."

"Live? Because I knew how to draw. I was real good at calligraphy, you know, artistic handwriting. My father insisted I learn that when I was young. It ended up saving my life."

"How?"

"Well, when I was at the hospital a lot of people were there, standing in line. I'm waiting, and out comes this man, another prisoner, and he asks, 'Anyone here know how to write? Anyone with good handwriting?' So I raised my hand, he took me over, and I wrote a few lines for him. I wrote two words, 'heart attack.' The Germans kept excellent records. Everybody who died had to have a cause of death. The cause was always the same: heart attack. That's all I wrote for hours—heart attack, heart attack, heart attack—always in beautiful script. Nobody was killed, they all died of heart attacks."

"So how did this . . .?"

"The man—he was a prisoner himself—gave me an extra bowl of soup from the bottom of the cauldron. You see, the Germans never stirred the soup, and the good stuff was always at the bottom. Whether you lived or died depended upon if you got soup from the top, which was just water, really, or soup from the bottom. But as it turned out, the soup was so salty I couldn't eat it. I cried uncontrollably over not being able to eat this soup. He saw me, tried it himself, and threw it out. Then he gave me two pieces of black bread.

"That saved my life, just a few pieces of bread. I'll never forget him, Stefan Heiman was his name. He saved my life by giving me bread and keeping me around to regain my strength for the next few days, without being sent out of the hospital. It's amazing, that's all you need really to get your strength back: just a few days and a little more food."

"Did you go back to working at the factory then?"

"No, he fixed it so I could stay at the hospital and be a record keeper. I stayed there until January, I think, January 1945. That's how I survived Auschwitz, by working in the camp hospital. I also worked as a nurse and got typhus. A friend saved my life by treating me, bathing me to keep my temperature down. And there's more to tell, but I think that . . ."

"Right," I cut him off. I needed to catch my breath.

The rest of Michel's story included his evacuation from Auschwitz, a death march for many of the prisoners, transport by cattle car to Buchenwald, and then to Berga, and finally from there on foot to another camp. It was during the march from Berga that he and two companions escaped; Michel, with a wound on his head from rifle fire. They lived on raw potatoes and tree bark in the woods until they found work with some local farmers and were hired as laborers for the planting season. After that Michel parted with his friends, left the farms to head west, and was picked up by American soldiers at a roadblock. He was put into a Prisoner of War camp with German soldiers, none of whom, fortunately, made any effort to find out who he was.

The Americans in charge of the camp did, of course, and were astonished to learn that he was not another runaway German soldier but a concentration camp survivor from Auschwitz.

"They looked at me as though I were from Mars," Michel concluded. "They couldn't believe that I was a prisoner there, so they asked me all about it. Questions, questions, questions." He paused. "Something like this, I guess."

His comment made me feel guilty.

"Mr. Michel, how did you end up here?"

"The Americans at the POW camp gave me some papers—you know, saying who I was and all that—and a motorcycle, and I took off to come home. It took me a long time, though—about two weeks. Roadblocks, wrecked bridges, bombed out roads—that sort of thing. Finally I got here and saw that everything had been bombed, destroyed; there was nothing left. I drove around on my motorcycle to the places I used to know, but everything is gone. And nobody knows anything about anyone. I kept driving around and asking, but it was no use, really. They're all gone.

"Your family . . .?"

"The last I heard from my parents was a note they sent me via the Red Cross. They said that all Jews from southern Germany went to a camp somewhere in France." He paused. "I think they're dead."

"Any brothers, sisters, Mr. Michel?" Hasselkorn asked.

"One sister, Lotte. She left in the early part of 1938 to live with a Jewish French family. But the Germans rounded up all the Jews in France, too, of course. I never heard from her." Another pause. "She's probably gone, too."

Neither Hasselkorn nor I knew what to say. Michel was surely right.

He finished his thought. "I guess there's no one left but me."

We were silent. He continued. "So I'm still driving around and night comes, and some American MPs pick me up and ask me why I'm still out—they say, there's a curfew, you know. I tell them I've got no place to go, so they send me to jail. I wasn't arrested or anything; I needed a place to sleep and they didn't know what else to do with me.

"The next day an American officer asks me what I'm going to do, that I can't just go driving around. I told him I don't know what I'm going to do, and he told me to come here. So that's what I did. I came into the building, and the first person I saw was . . ."

Michel looked at Hasselkorn, at his lapel insignia with the Ten Commandments. For the first time since I'd seen him, he smiled.

". . . the chaplain. And he takes me to you. So . . . here I am. Can you tell me what to do? I can speak other languages, French, some Czech and Polish, Yiddish, a little English. I'm a good artist, I can do calligraphy. I really don't want to do that again. But I can translate."

"You don't have a place to live, do you," I said. It was not a question.

"No."

"Let's fix that right now. Come with me, Mr. Michel. Abe. Let's go on a trip."

The three of us left my office. Hasselkorn asked, "Where are we going?"

"To the only place in Mannheim that hasn't been leveled," I said.

On our way out of the building we breezed by the two American sergeants from the Public Safety Section who I had assisted earlier that day during their interrogation of the former Nazi *Gauleiter*.

"Lieutenant?" one of them asked.

"Later," I said.

We hopped into my jeep and rumbled along the dusty roads until we arrived in a quiet, residential section untouched by the war. I stopped the jeep in front of a row of houses and turned to Michel.

"Which one do you want?"

Michel gave me a questioning look. "I can live in one of those houses?"

"Yeah. Now, which one do you want?"

Still not sure, he looked over the neighborhood, a house at a time.

"I don't know, sir. One house looks as good to me as another."

I picked a house close to us. "How about that one?"

"Sure, that's fine."

"Good. Stay here in the jeep."

I hopped out of the vehicle, marched to the house, and pounded on the door. It opened and a man stood there with his hand on the door handle. Before he could speak, I said, "I am requisitioning this house for the Seventh Army Displaced Persons Section. You are hereby ordered to leave. Now!"

He was too stunned to respond. At that time no one argued with an American army officer. Within five minutes, he and several other occupants of the house left, and I went to Michel, still in the jeep, and turned the house over to him.

"Here," I said, hastily signing a piece of paper and handing it to him. "This authorizes you to live in this house. You can report to my office tomorrow and work as my interpreter and assistant. OK?"

Michel nodded his head slowly and smiled with appreciation. This time it was his turn to be astonished.

"Thank you, sir. Thank you, sir," he said, looking first at me, then at Hasselkorn. "You know, this is . . . quite a coincidence."

"How's that?" Hasselkorn asked.

"It's my birthday today."

"Your birthday?" we said together.

"Yes. I'm twenty-two today." He scanned the dimensions of the house, then walked toward it. He turned by the door and said, "Thank you, thank you again. I will see you tomorrow, then."

"Yes, tomorrow," I said.

When Hasselkorn and I returned to the office building, I found two sergeants from the Public Safety Section waiting to talk with me. Hasselkorn went off, and I invited them into my office. They quickly told me their story.

"You left him with his what?" I asked.

"His belt, I'm afraid. We had no idea he would hang himself, sir; it just happened. Frankly, I didn't think about it at all. The question is, what should we do now?"

For a long moment I said nothing.

Gather five million belts and hand them out to every Gauleiter in Germany, I answered silently. *Let 'em all hang themselves.*

"Lieutenant?"

"Contact the Public Safety Section immediately and tell them what happened. I'll call them up and see what I can do," I said.

"OK, Lieutenant. Thank you."

"That will be all."

"Yes sir."

The sergeants left and I sat there alone, doing nothing. After a moment or so I got up, walked toward the window and stared at the city, at the part of Mannheim that Hasselkorn and I had just left.

Happy birthday Ernest Wolfgang Michel, I said to myself. *Happy birthday.*

Our American Military Government Counseling Service

The addition of Michel to my staff was an excellent one. His work complemented that of Paul Venneker, a dashing young Dutchman who had survived a German labor camp and spoke French, German, English, and Dutch (of course), along with a smattering of Polish. He had passed our *fragebogen* (questionnaire) test, which cleared him of any prior association with the Nazis. Between Venneker, Michel, Sergeant Weiss, and myself, we nicely covered the range of European languages we needed to work with, excepting Russian. In fact, I was relieved to get him when we did, especially in light of the person he replaced.

Venneker's forerunner, a stiff, distinguished looking German, had pranced into my office in the early days of our occupation to offer us his services. At first I thought a jewel had dropped in our laps. His command of several languages was impressive, and he knew the provinces of Baden and Württemberg well. Although he denied any association with the Nazis, his behavior quickly belied these disclaimers. My unit's mission was to service the needs of DPs and Jews, but our haughty volunteer quickly showed that he had different priorities: he allowed only well-dressed Germans, Austrians, or Western Europeans into my office and coolly rejected the approaches of anyone else. Finally, when he let a comment slip about how the Germans and Americans would soon be allied to fight against the Russians—a stock piece of German propaganda at the time—I decided to investigate. When I discovered that he had never filled out our questionnaire, I ordered him to do so. The results revealed several past Nazi affiliations, and he was immediately arrested and jailed.

Our interpreter had upheld his status only briefly, and only because we were able to "smoke him out" in our office. Establishing one's status had become of paramount importance for the residents of Mannheim, because it affected how the occupation authorities dealt with them. For instance, one well-dressed, middle-aged German claimed "Jewish" status, apparently assuming that Jews would be treated better than Germans. He entered my office, stood at attention, clicked his heels, announced his name, and bowed smartly like a Prussian.

"Of Jewish 'extraction,' you say?" I asked.

"Jawohl, Herr Commandant."

My God, here's another one, I thought.

"I have been living in Mannheim all my life. I am married to a Christian woman of quality for twenty years. I renounced my Judaism upon marriage."

"Yet you claim to be a Jew. If you are a Jew, why did the Nazis leave you alone?"

"They didn't. My wife was not allowed to shop before four o'clock in the afternoon, and the shops were always out of food by then. And I never knew when there might be a midnight knock on the door, when they might come to take me away to a camp."

"But you still managed to stay out of a camp. Why?"

He answered proudly, "I believe it was because of my wife's family and my standing in the community. But as I said, they made us suffer in other ways. I must add that I represent others who are in a position similar to mine. We are wondering about our treatment under American military occupation."

I was skeptical of his case. "Did the SS ever bother you, search you, threaten you? Did the Gestapo ever make it clear you were on a list?"

His answer came slowly. "No, not exactly."

"Well, how exactly were you treated? Were your children taken? Any of your family? Was your house confiscated? Did you ever work in a labor camp?"

"No . . . those things didn't happen."

"Were you made to suffer in any way?"

"There were shortages, of course."

"Shortages affected everyone," I cut in. "I want to know if you were singled out in any way, persecuted, beyond what you've mentioned?"

No . . . no, not actually."

"Then I must inform you that you will be treated just as any other German national."

Although he couldn't mask his chagrin, the German didn't try to argue with me. He simply bowed, said, "*danke*," clicked his heels, did a correct about-face, and left my office. I never heard from him or any of his group again.

His desire to attain "Jewish" status was well founded. American army directives allowed German nationals who had Jewish parents or grandparents to keep their homes without fear of confiscation. Thus, it was not surprising that many Germans tried hard to ferret out such relationships in their ancestry—an ironic twist to situations of those with Jewish backgrounds in years past. Some even put together papers to document their case, but few could actually prove any Jewish ancestry.

Others tried to establish their DP status as Jews to hold onto the few possessions they had. Our Public Safety Section usually investigated such claims. Sometimes they were genuine; sometimes not. The claims turned down occasionally involved former Nazis who tried to conceal their past to prevent arrest and incarceration. One such case involved a group of men, twenty-two in all, who came to me requesting DP status so they could retain use of an abandoned apartment house they were living in and secure medical care, food, and clothing. I sent them to the Public Safety Section, where eighteen showed up; of that number, three were discovered as having had Nazi party connections. The arrogance they showed in thinking they could get away with such a ruse appalled me. They ended up in jail.

An even more galling case involved a Polish Catholic family of seven, who took considerable risk to complain to my office about their German employer. They had worked for him as forced labor for a year. He had provided them with an apartment and food, but no wages. After American occupation authorities took over the city, they asked him for wages as well and were promptly fired and kicked out of their apartment for their trouble. I advised that we resolve this matter in my office and ordered their German boss to appear at 1100 hours with me and the family. We waited until noon, but he never showed up. Finally, I sent Sergeant Weiss out to get him.

"Why didn't you report? You received our order, did you not?"

He looked at me with casual disdain. "Yes, I did," he said.

"So why didn't you come? Surely you know the way."

"I knew the way. Of course, I knew the way. I've lived in Mannheim all my life."

Sharply, I said, "We expected you to be here."

He responded with a flippant, almost bored look. "I was not finished working in my garden."

"What?"

"Frankly, I didn't think a request from an American lieutenant was all that important. And I was busy; I'm a busy man. I don't have time for this sort of thing. That's all."

I made no effort to suppress my anger. "You will not find yourself too busy to do *this* 'sort of thing,' mister." I nodded in the direction of the parents of the family, who were with us in the office, and said, "They will return to their apartment immediately."

His eyebrows raised, but only slightly.

"You will rehire them and pay them the current wage."

He stiffened, trying to contain his indignation as I spelled out the consequences of his arrogance, one point at a time.

"And you will be placed in jail pending trial on charges of showing disrespect for officials of the American Military Government. Is that clear?"

The German stood before me, erect, arms down to his sides, the insolence drained from his bearing. He could not suppress a look of surprise; however, it faded to one of contempt as he turned, directed by an American soldier who was thoroughly enjoying the spectacle, and left my office. I sat through his trial with satisfaction. He received a ninety-day jail sentence, a fine of ten thousand marks, and a court order to reimburse the family for back wages, in addition to the penalties I had announced in my office. Sometimes there was satisfaction in retribution.

Not all Germans were like that, of course, and there were several cases of "righteous Christians" that warmed our hearts. One involved a countess from Heidelberg who had concealed the identity of a young Jewish girl from Poland. She had secured false identification papers for her, given her a cross to wear, and retained her as a maid for over a year. But now the countess was in difficult straits, and her ward requested food and other assistance from the AMG. I agreed and ordered provisions for them both, as if they were DPs. Another case involved a German farmer who had kept a concentration camp escapee on his farm as a worker, hiding him in the attic whenever the authorities came by. The boy asked that the farmer be given a pass to travel for his supplies beyond the ten-kilometer limit set by occupation authorities. He received it, as well as a letter of commendation from the AMG.

Without question, the most dramatic and emotional times at the office involved reunions, especially those that occurred on "Jewish Day," which was every Wednesday afternoon. During these times, Jews were free to wander into my office to discuss their problems with me and Chaplain Hasselkorn. Sometimes we were faced with the outcomes of decisions I had made weeks or months earlier.

One day I entered my office and walked into an enthusiastic embrace from a bright-eyed young man.

"Lieutenant Hutler!"

"Uh, yes." I was deep in thought, concentrating on a handful of documents. His greeting had startled me.

"We have come back to see you, to thank you." There were five other men in the room, all of them with worn faces smiling, happy to see me. I returned their smiles, but could not instantly place them. Having dealt with hundreds, thousands, of people and their problems, I occasionally needed a moment's thought to bring the specifics to the forefront. They spoke Polish. Michel was hurried in from his reception desk to translate.

One of them held up an object and waved it. It was a small sheath of papers, encased in eisenglass for protection. The items were not letters; the papers looked official.

"We made it back," another said, "and we wanted to see you before we went anywhere else. Your papers worked like magic. Everybody helped us."

"I see. Well, good. Excellent." Their faces came back to me; the details of an action I had taken a month ago trickled back into my mind. "What happened? Did you make it where you wanted to go?"

"Yes," said the spokesman, the one who had hugged me. "Thanks to these." He handed me the encased documents. They had an AMG letterhead on the top and my signature on the bottom:

> Notice:
>
> The bearer of this letter, a Jewish survivor of a concentration camp, is attempting to return to his former home in Poland to search for surviving members of his family. Please render him any assistance you can, with the appreciation of AMG Seventh Army detachment

F1E2 Co. E2 ECAR. [Signed] Lieutenant Albert A. Hutler

"This gave us an open door across the American zone. We got rides from truck drivers and stayed in American army barracks. American soldiers fed us and helped us along."

This was comforting—warm impressions of American soldiers, memories they would never forget. They had come to my office with no passports, no travel documents, no identification of any sort, and no money. I had sent them off with those identifying letters, and American soldiers helped them on their way. But the bravery of these Polish Jews overshadowed any assistance we gave them. Traveling across three international boundaries, each guarded heavily by armed troops, they had risked their lives to see if any of their families had survived. Their hometown was Radom.

"Did you find any of your families or relatives?"

The answer came slowly. "No, no . . . , we did not."

"Are you going back, then?"

"No," the speaker looked around him, and met his friends' eyes. "We do not want to go back to walk on the bones and blood of our families and friends."

Michel nodded his head and slowly closed and opened his eyes, silently acknowledging the comment. I said nothing.

"So!" The word cracked the silence, signaling an end to the visit. "Now we must be going. But we wanted thank you for your help, you and the chaplain, and the Americans, all of you!"

Another hug, followed by six more, and the Polish Jews filed out of my office to find another place to spend their lives, probably in Palestine or America. They left me depressed, and I think Michel was, too, although he was never the kind to give up hope. He departed quietly, without a word.

It was early evening. I looked at the documents I had carried into the room with me. Pushing them aside, I took out a clean sheet of paper and picked up a pen. After today's visitors, yesterday's, last week's, my mind was full, bursting. Time to write my wife.

My Dearest Leanore,

Wednesday is Jewish day at my office. This is the day that Jews who are displaced gather to tell their stories to the chaplain and me. It is the day when they may open their hearts, when they are able to talk, when they feel that they are again free. It is, however, a day when Chaplain Hasselkorn and I suffer...

At yesterday's meeting, a man with a record of six years at Buchenwald, with its "standing room," its "incinerator," the "small camp," a man broken in body and yet with hope—hope because he has a sister in England and a cousin in America—came to the office. He talked of his own daughters who, he heard, are in a camp in the Russian area. His eyes glow as he speaks, and yet he does not know whether they are alive or dead. He speaks gently of his wife, whom the Nazis murdered. What can we do for him? A pair of shoes, a suit, a few suits of underwear, a shirt—we can give him these. But can the Germans be made to give him back his wife, his girls, or even his healthy body? America just won't believe.

I saw a handsome boy of sixteen years with two years of his life lost in Buchenwald. He looks as if he

> cannot believe he is free. I can't forget the face of the girl who left five years of her life in Dachau. These things are so hard to believe—they are so hard to understand.

Michel drifted into my reflections, his survival, his evacuation from Auschwitz, the Germans' efforts to cover up what they had done before the Russians came thundering in from the east, before the Americans and British uncovered Nazi barbarisms in the west. My mind turned off for a moment, exhausted. I just sat there.

Then, slowly, thoughts came forth, like a gradual rise in the volume of a radio, and became more distinct, clear. Michel, the Radom Jews, the uncovered graves, smoke up the chimney—atrocity after atrocity.

They had to know what they were doing was evil. Otherwise, why go to the trouble to cover it up?

I was convinced—I still am convinced—that God implanted in every human being a foundation of morality that commands what is right and what is wrong. Even the worst monstrosities of modern thought cannot totally succeed in eradicating this ground of moral conviction. The Nazis chose to do evil deeds. They chose evil, knowing the good.

If they truly believed their actions were morally justified, then there was no reason to try to conceal them before the judgment of the world.

I continued with the letter:

> I can't understand these Germans. One Sunday I was amazed to see many of them carrying flowers;

> beautiful, colorful tulips and lilacs. They fondled them lovingly. How can people love beautiful things and still kill as they have done? How can they fondle the lovely straight lines of a tulip, and still lovingly fondle the button which starts the gas in a death chamber where thousands of people have been killed? How can they smell the lovely scents of the lilac with the same nose that has smelled out the Jew in order to torture and kill him for being a Jew? What kind of mentality did God put into the bodies, into the heads of these human beings, to make them love flowers but hate the human race?

I didn't know how to end this letter. After a moment's reflection, I wrote:

> Wednesday will always be Jewish day for me!

With that last thought, I closed the office and went to my quarters.

About a month after the Polish Jews visited me, I was greeted with another eastern European delegation: this time, twenty-seven young women, all Hungarian Jews, hungry, tired, and haggard, with Auschwitz numbers burned on their arms. They had been hiding in a forest for almost two months and came dressed in American GI uniforms, which were filthy and ragged. They asked for clean clothing, food, and shelter. They needed to be deloused and cleaned up before we could figure out what to do with them. I had them trucked to Kaiser Wilhelm Kaserne and later to our warehouse, where they picked up enough personal items—such as toothbrushes and toothpaste—to last them for a short period.

A few weeks later, I was greeted by six soldiers of the Jewish Brigade, a part of the British military forces. They had eight of these girls with them.

"Yes, I'm familiar with the Jewish Brigade," I said. "It's a pleasure to have you here."

"Thank you, sir," said their spokesman.

"Could you tell me what these young ladies are doing here with you?"

"Yes sir. They're our cousins. We tracked them down through the locater system and then traveled to your DP camp and picked them up."

"I see." I'd heard of stranger things. "So how can I help you."

"We would appreciate getting transportation to Hamburg, sir. We can then ship them to Palestine."

"I can arrange that." I buzzed Sergeant Weiss to secure a truck from the motor pool and enough provisions for their trip and stay in Hamburg. I also assigned him to drive the truck.

"Thank you very much, Lieutenant."

"You're welcome," I said. I was glad to have a request I could handle so quickly and completely.

"By the way," he said, standing by the door, ready to leave. "Do you happen to know an Ernest Michel?"

I perked up. "Why do you want to know?"

"I have a letter here that I've been carrying for him."

"Where is it from?"

"Palestine."

"How is it that you're carrying a letter from Palestine?"

"Through the Central Committee of Jewish Survivors.

One of their members asked me to see if I could find him. There's someone in Palestine who's trying to reach him."

I didn't know Ernst had any contacts with anyone in Palestine.

The soldier continued, "Apparently this person got a package containing a pair of shoes from a friend in the American zone. The shoes were wrapped in a Displaced Persons newspaper put out by the Jewish survivors' group, and it had a list of survivors and where they might be living. She noticed Mr. Michel's name when she was unwrapping the shoes and wrote him this letter. Is he here?"

"Yes, he is, I'll get him," I said, and dashed out to grab Michel from the reception office. We hurried back to my office, and I introduced him to the soldier. He repeated his explanation quickly and handed Ernest the letter.

Michel eyed the paper with quiet anxiety. He opened it carefully and slowly began to read. I stood there with the soldier, mute, frozen.

Michel grasped the letter tightly. His hand began to tremble; his eyes became moist, then welled with tears.

"What is it, Ernest!"

Droplets trickled down his cheeks.

"My sister," he said with a shaky voice, his eyes still riveted to the paper. "My sister Lotte. She's alive."

I felt a lump in my throat. His face became blurry.

Then, looking up at me directly, "She's alive, Lieutenant. She's ALIVE!"

We embraced, squeezing each other and wiping our wet faces with our sleeves. Time stood still for a moment, with the comforting warmth of joy and peace.

Chapter Three

From Death Camp To A Castle: The Radom Jews

An Unintended Adoption

Chaplain Hasselkorn entered my office and coughed politely to get my attention. I looked up to see a worried expression on his face. More than that, he gave me a look that I knew from past experience would somehow make my day more complicated.

"Have you ever heard of the Jews of Radom?" he asked.

I mentally thumbed through our nationalities list. French, Dutch, Italians, Greeks, Belgians, and Luxembourgians—

most of them were in their home countries now, although a few hundred still managed to show up now and then. There was a vast assortment of eastern Europeans—Russians, Poles, Ukrainians, Lithuanians, Estonians, Rumanians, Yugoslavians, and Hungarians—many of whom were terrified to go home, but had no choice. Then there were the Jews, from all over Europe—most of them couldn't go home because they had none or were fearful of returning to what had been their homes in other lands before the war. But among this polyglot assemblage of displaced persons, I had to admit that I had not heard of this particular group of people, the Jews of Radom. Hasselkorn proceeded to inform me.

"I've been in contact with the French commander of a DP camp near Neuenberg. The German population was evacuated, and there are around 250 survivors of the Vaihingen concentration camp living there now."

Evacuation of German inhabitants to provide accommodations for DPs was not an unusual procedure. Since late March our orders had been to rummage the area to find homes for displaced persons, a practice that occasionally involved relieving some Germans of their own comfortable abodes. Considering the immense suffering they had caused others, hardly anyone considered this an injustice.

"How many were in the concentration camp originally?" I asked.

"About three thousand."

"How are they doing? How are the French handling it?"

"The DPs are recovering, but they're still in pretty bad shape, and the French are doing their best. The French Red Cross is there, and the whole group has more or less been adopted by a really charming lady." Hasselkorn paused for a moment. "A Madame Vaison, I think, is her name. She's a real saint. She loves them, she's doing a tremendous job, and they all love her. But she can only do so much, and when I visited, about half of the group was bedridden with typhus. The worst part is that the French commander has been ordered to put them in a Polish DP camp, and they're very afraid of that."

There was good reason for that fear. Many of the DP camps were notorious for their anti-Semitism, and Polish camps were among the worst. Although the Jews had been liberated from the death camps, they still had to cope with the centuries' old legacy of hatred against them, which had been powerfully exacerbated, of course, by the Nazis' policies in their conquered lands. For many of them, the war was still not over.

"What is it? Do they want our help or something?" I inquired. "Supplies, medics, or what?"

Hasselkorn sat down uncomfortably. "Actually, they didn't ask for anything, or not exactly." He paused. "But I'm asking you for something."

I gave him a puzzled look.

"I'm wondering if we could bring these people into our area, to set up our own camp for them. We've got camps for every other nationality around, and none of them is as bad off as the Radom Jews. The French commander is worried about what's going to happen to them if they get sent to a Polish camp, and it would take a burden off his shoulders if we helped him out. I met him the other day, and he seems like an understanding guy."

I shifted in my chair uneasily. "I doubt that we can do that, Abe. We're loaded with what we already have. Housing's short—overcrowding everywhere—and Jewish DPs always need more care than the others." My own review discouraged me. "I just don't think we can help them—unless you know something I don't."

"How about a separate section in one of the existing camps?"

I shook my head. "There's just no room. Besides, that just gives us the same problem the French have. They wouldn't be any better off here than they would be elsewhere."

He stared at me, dissatisfied, unconvinced. My skepticism was justified, but he remained unmoved. I tried to fend off his look by repeating what usually constitutes the final word on such matters: "Besides, regulations are against it. There can be no transfer of DPs between occupation zones."

Hasselkorn gave me a sideways glance, with a playful grin on his face. "I've never known you to be a stickler for regulations."

"Only if they make sense," I replied.

Like all officers, I did my best to respect the endless outpouring of army regulations, directives, manuals, orders, and whatnot, with all their myriad rescissions, supersessions, deletions, additions, and whatever other terms the army's clerical geniuses dreamed up to explain ad hoc changes in policy. But regulations occasionally conflicted with one another or left some situations undefined, and sometimes commanders were not aware of the rules that other officers, with different responsibilities, had to observe. For instance, by inclination and training, combat officers were rarely concerned with DP problems. Their job was hard, brutal; they had no time or patience to deal with the victims of war. I understood this, but I still had to cope with the problems their insensitive approach sometimes created.

One situation, perhaps the one Hasselkorn currently had in mind, involved my advising the commanding general of the Sixty-third Division of my determination to go over his head, if necessary, to get one of his orders changed. The issue came up when a military police (MP) unit from his division entered Mannheim during my absence and ordered DPs out of private dwellings (apartments and homes) and into the Kaiser Wilhelm Kaserne, our main camp. This action not only swelled the population of the camp to dangerous and unmanageable proportions but also threw the Polish Jewish survivors into an environment that contained many vicious anti-Semites. It was my job to protect all camp inmates, and because of my experience and training, I was constantly sensitive to such matters. The infantry general thought differently.

But I also felt strongly that his action and my response represented more than just conflicting responsibilities or different perspectives. My staff had told me that the MPs had conducted the moves callously. At gunpoint, they had prodded frightened, confused residents out of their living quarters and herded them onto trucks and out to the barracks, even leaving some nursing infants behind in abandoned rooms. The order struck my AMG section as nasty, unthinking, unwarranted, and its implementation, brutal, almost Nazi-like. Further, it was contrary to Supreme Headquarters Allied Expeditionary Forces (SHAEF) policy on dealing with DPs, a point I repeated with indelicate insistence.

Naturally, such outspokenness is not the recommended way to stay on good terms with the higher brass. My own commander, Colonel Winning, was also present at that meeting, and he was sternly warned that if I were under the general's command, I would be court-martialed for insubordination—a reasonable enough conclusion. The colonel remarked that it was fortunate for me that I was not under the general's command—with which I silently and heartily agreed—and then dismissed me. I wondered what Colonel Winning would say about the Radom Jews' situation.

Hasselkorn was insistent. "Come on, Al, why don't you just see them."

"See them, you say."

"Yeah, see them, talk with them, listen to them, hear their stories, you know. That's not asking too much."

Obviously, he was not going to take no for an answer. "All right, I'll be able to make it up there in a few days. They're not being shipped out immediately, are they?"

"No, a few days would be OK."

I nodded in agreement and then went back to my business.

I took the trip to Neuenberg with Sergeant Weiss, chatting with him about our options as we traveled in our jeep over the bumpy roads.

"It would be great 'mitzvah' [good deeds], Lieutenant, if we could bring them into our area."

"I know it would. But I don't see how it's possible."

"Great 'mitzvah'," he repeated.

I countered by bringing up the same objections I had gone over with Hasselkorn, concluding again that it was impossible. Still, our trip was dominated by discussing the ramifications of this clear "impossibility."

At least we were not bothered by any remaining snipers in the area, even though it was well past V-E Day. While visiting the DP camps in the Mannheim region, it was our usual practice to race our jeep pell-mell over the roads through the woods and outlying areas, which were sometimes dangerous, and then onto the autobahn. Fortunately, our thirty-mile trip into the French zone of occupation was not disturbed by any pointless attempts on the part of some demented Wehrmacht soldier to effect his solitary revenge upon the occupying troops.

When we arrived at the village in the French zone, we found the commander there fully as personable and cooperative as Hasselkorn had said he was. I knew a little French and did not really need Weiss's services to determine that the captain was genuinely concerned about the Radom Jews. With accompanying gestures, he declared that they were recovering quite well, had given him no trouble, and that his orders to move them out had caused them all great consternation.

"It is a great injustice, but those are my orders," he reiterated, a bit formally. "They're doing well now, but many won't make it in a Polish camp."

"I understand," I said. "May we see them?"

"Certainly," he said approvingly. Then he gave us some simple directions. "To the center of the village." A wan, but earnest and knowing smile passed across his face. "You will see them if you drive to the center of the village."

"Thank you, Captain." After saluting, Weiss and I got

into our jeep and slowly drove down the main street of Neuenberg.

We stopped at a point that seemed near the center of the village. Neuenberg consisted of a series of small mortar and brick houses along with numerous frame buildings, all closely huddled together under steep roofs. Several structures had stucco facades smartly outlined with wood framing, windows graced with shutters and flower boxes, yards filled with well-tended vegetable gardens and cleanly trimmed lawns. The town was the very picture of a classic, quaint German village. It had a storybook charm that fortunately had been spared from the ravages that had leveled so many other places like it.

For an indeterminate time, we just sat in the jeep and looked around, pondering how to approach the situation. The weather was warm; the sky, clear; the air, clean and fulsome—it was a beautiful day. And there we sat, wondering what our next move should be.

"So, what do we do now?" Weiss asked.

I had no good answer. "For the moment, just wait, I guess."

Finally, we got out of the jeep and started to walk toward several of the cottages, our heads turning in this direction and that, looking for some sign of movement. Then, after moments of silence and hesitation, we had our first meeting with the Jews of Radom. Images of people, partially concealed by the wispy shadows of faintly illuminated rooms, appeared behind some windows—a glance here, a hand there, slowly pulling aside a curtain. Curious, nervous eyes surveyed us from behind doors, windows, and corners, observing, evaluating these two American soldiers standing before them. Several figures then appeared in full and began to walk toward us, slowly and haltingly. They were soon joined by others, and before too long a circle of men had formed around us, one hundred and fifty individuals in all, over half of the survivors of the Vaihingen concentration camp, the last death camp for the Jews of Radom.

Absolutely nothing can prepare one for the sight of a concentration camp survivor. No "normal" human reactions can compare with the incredulity, shock, and utter incomprehension felt when encountering human beings like these. Their relationship to the world of the living seemed more tenuous than even our fleeting shadows. "Skin and bones" is the usual description applied to survivors of death camps, and it aptly fit these people as well; none of the grown men before us weighed more than seventy or seventy-five pounds. Indeed, their faces appeared as ghastly apparitions—dark, sunken eyes, hollow cheeks, and pallid skin drawn taut over grayish teeth that were etched in black lines among colorless gums. And these were just a few among the thousands who had been liberated from concentration camps all over Europe.

Everyone knew, of course, about the Nazi death camps. We were familiar with how some Nazi camp guards, with a grotesque meticulousness peculiar to their kind, would often place bodies scheduled for burial or cremation on the horse-drawn carts so that the heads and feet alternated, in order to maximize available space. Yet when I looked at the men around me, I was gripped with the feeling that the only thing that separated them from the wretched "cargo" on those carts, filled with bony, desiccated bodies with their gaping mouths and visionless stares, was a single, solitary breath. They had escaped the agony of death, only to encounter the agony of survival.

For many their survival was symbolized by the prison garb they still wore—the striped suits of death camp inmates, now filthy, ragged, and odorous—which they treated as though they were a badge of honor. Several of them dressed this way approached us, their scrubby faces conveying a sense of desperation: *"Zint yer a Yid?"* one asked. *"Zint yer a Rebbe?"* questioned another. I had once been fluent in Yiddish, but years of disuse rendered me incapable of providing little more than short answers to their queries.

"Yes, we're Jewish," I answered. "But we are not rabbis. I am Lieutenant Hutler, and this is Sergeant Weiss—United States Army."

We were the only American Jewish soldiers that they had ever seen, with the exception of Chaplain Hasselkorn. They remembered his uniform well. His visit had obviously made an enormous impression, and the survivors warmed up to us immediately. Their faces, coarsely weathered by the horrors of the past, now softened with a disarming radiance. They pressed closer and embraced us, kissed our hands, and proclaimed us their brothers and their friends.

Then the men's stories poured out—accounts of their experiences in the Vaihingen concentration camp. "Day and night we slaved, cutting stone and tile," recounted one striped-suit survivor. "We were forced to carry the stone on our backs eighteen hours a day. Men dropped dead from the strain. Nobody knew what happened to the stone that so many had died to cut and to carry. If we dared to ask them, they just laughed and said that it was for our own crematorium."

Another, also wearing a prison uniform, offered this story: "Yes, for ten months I lived there; ten months with a stone on my back. I walked back and forth in the quarry, all day and half the night. I remember falling down many times and lying there, wanting to be dead. Then they whipped me, forcing me to get up. If you did not get up, they shot you on the spot. Many were shot. I don't know how I went on living." A whisper of pride softly adorned his last statement: "But I am here now, I made it!"

"But there's not many left," came another voice.

"At first there were 3,000 men from Radom," someone else said. "Then later there were about 2,300. Now there are only 249 left."

"All my male relatives were there with me," a voice from the back offered. "Shall I tell you how many there were?"

Silence.

"No, I shall not." He paused. "I was the only one left in the end."

The stories continued to gush out: "We couldn't sleep," one of them said. "They put us on bunks one on top of the other so we could hardly breathe. Sometimes we hid in a dark tunnel in order to sleep without the searchlights in our eyes. Now and then the guards would come in and poke around with their torches. They shot you if they caught you there."

And on they went, each one opening up to us his innermost thoughts, the terrifying nightmares of day-to-day existence in the death camp. One of them—their leader, it turned out—paid us an extraordinary compliment. His name was Marek Guttman.

"None of us thought we could talk about what happened to us." he said. "We thought we would go mad if we did so. But we could talk to the chaplain [Hasselkorn]. You are like the chaplain. We can talk to you, too. We can unburden ourselves."

He also filled in the account given by another inmate about the camp's liberation: "When the French came in, we rushed out of the barbed wire area to see them. The field around us was covered with stacks of bodies, piled up on top of one another in layers, like sacks of potatoes. All day we looked into the piles, everyone seeking his own kin. Whenever it was possible to identify someone, we placed his name over a makeshift grave."

Guttman continued the story, explaining how the Radom Jews, with emaciated bodies and ravaged souls, had valiantly attempted to provide their loved ones with some simple but beautiful adornments to commemorate their deaths, to lend dignity to these departed children of God. They had survived all that, I thought, only to be faced with the prospect of being moved out again to a place that filled their hearts with foreboding.

Many were terrified of going to a Polish DP camp. "It would be a gift," one said, "to go with you, American Jews. We could live together like a Jewish family. Yes! A Jewish family!" They begged us to take them with us, to go with the Americans, to begin their lives again in safety, in peace, and in happiness; as one them said, like one big, happy Jewish family.

I wasn't prepared for this. I had agreed to go to Neuenberg because Hasselkorn had insisted, and Weiss and I had chatted about our options on the trip to the village. But I lacked authority and I had resolved not to take any official action; the Radom Jews were in a different occupation zone. None of that seemed to matter now. My earlier decision to do nothing but look and see had vanished, swept away by the impact of their stories, by their desperate pleas for our help. My body was covered with sweat, and I was cold all over. Weiss and I looked at each other, and then away again. He was in no better shape than I was.

I was more than just physically uncomfortable. I didn't like the way they made me feel. Since early April, my unit had received, fed, clothed, bedded down, and shipped out thousands of people, tens of thousands, on a daily basis. But they were masses; I got to know some of them, but not many. The people before me were individuals; their situation became personal. And they were all looking at me, Al Hutler, making me feel like God. But I was only a lieutenant in the United States Army, and somehow I didn't think that was fair.

I turned my head and shut my eyes. When I opened them, my vision met the pleading stare of the last speaker.

Not fair? Compared to what?

With my throat constricted, I tried to maintain some semblance of official composure and muttered something like, "Yes, well, every effort will be made to bring you into the American zone." Official? Impersonal? Ridiculous!

What followed was a scene involving scores of concentration camp survivors showering two American soldiers with as much gratitude as their frail bodies could manage. I felt that even a token acknowledgment of their thanks would put a dangerous strain on my efforts to maintain self-control. I nodded, swallowed hard a few times, accepted their thanks, but said very little. In fact, I said nothing at all. But I knew that from that time forward the Jews of Radom would become "my Jews." I had unintentionally adopted a large Jewish family.

The Road to *Schloss Langenzelle*

I later learned that "my Jews" were among the very few survivors of what was once a proud and thriving center of Jewish culture in the city of Radom, Poland. Its population, then numbering around forty thousand, supported some one hundred tanneries and allied industries, which provided most of Poland's needs. Ceramics and iron ore industries also flourished, supplying markets as far away as Africa and South America. A large railway complex, with lines running east to Russia and north and west to Germany and the Baltic ports, transported the city's products. But these commercial and industrial activities were ancillary to the city's Jewish cultural foundation, which included an extensive network of hospitals, centers of learning, and publishing establishments for newspapers and books. In short, Radom was one of the stars in the galaxy of Jewish cultural centers in Poland before the war.

All this was changed by the German invasion in September 1939. As a result of Nazi deportations and mass murder, only three thousand persons remained in Radom, as slave laborers in a munitions factory when the Germans retreated in the summer of 1944. Others had previously escaped to join guerrilla units; some of these were even involved in the great Warsaw uprising of August 1944. But most had been killed by the Germans, and the few who remained were force-marched out of Poland to the Vaihingen concentration camp near Stuttgart, where they were left to die of a typhus epidemic. Of that number, only 249 remained when the camp was liberated by the French on April 7, 1945.[1] Their numbers were increased by other Jews who had initially returned to Poland after V-E Day, only to come back to a Western occupation zone because they could not survive the vicious anti-Semitism in their former "native" land. Thus, by one route or another, many Polish Jews found themselves at the mercy of the Western occupiers.

Such was the larger background of our immediate predicament, which was to find a way to move 249 Jewish DPs from one military zone of occupation to another. After our meeting with the Radom Jews, Weiss and I returned to the French commander's office to see what arrangements could be made. I was in an awkward position: I wanted to save them from a Polish DP camp, but I didn't want to show the commander my eagerness to relieve him of his responsibilities.

We thus haggled over the fate of human lives as though they were so many pieces of merchandise. It seemed that every action had a price—I'll do this if you'll do that. In the

---

[1]This information comes from Alfred Lipson, "Book of Radom," United Radom Relief Society of U.S. and Canada, published in New York, 1963.

end we agreed that I would take them off his hands if he would supply bedding and two days rations. Further, I agreed to supply the trucks to transport them from the French zone to the American zone, and he consented to have Madame Vaison assigned to us on temporary duty to help out. The deal was made. Now began the harder part: what on earth was I going to do with an additional 249 people in an area already saturated with DPs? Moreover, how was I going to explain my actions to my own commander?

One crisis at a time, I figured. During the next few days, we scoured the area around Mannheim until we found a small school building outside Bensheim, a town about fifteen miles from our headquarters in Mannheim and close to another one of our DP camps. I immediately requisitioned the structure from the German authorities and enlisted the help of local Germans to clean the place up and do the extensive repair work. My unit, frankly, drove them hard, and they worked frantically.

The workers converted classrooms into bedrooms, lounging areas, and medical rooms, set up a dining hall, and upgraded the kitchen facilities. They knocked down walls and built some additional ones, repainted the new and redecorated the old. We obtained furniture from nearby German homes and stores, stocked the kitchen with food, and graced the windows with flowers. I wanted to create a spotlessly clean environment for the Radom Jews, one filled with security, warmth, and good cheer.

Our visitors richly rewarded our efforts. The tour of their new surroundings left many speechless and all of them filled with wonder, joy, and gratitude. Everything around them exuded lightness, cleanliness, sylvan beauty, and the comforting warmth of the first truly secure living quarters any had experienced since the beginning of the war. The occasion culminated with their first meal in the American zone: a splendid Polish-Jewish repast, complete with hot potatoes and vegetables, "Jewish penicillin" (noodle soup), *kugel* (a kind of pudding), tea, coffee, and plenty of chocolate—all prepared by the German women from Bensheim. It was a superb inauguration to a new life.

Most of all, of course, they were free. They could come and go as they pleased, enjoy good meals served at regular intervals, sleep in the comfort of undisturbed peace, and wake with the optimism and hope of a shining new dawn. But this was just their first stopover in the American zone; others would follow. And I was wondering if it would be my last action on their behalf, for I had yet to inform my superior, Colonel Winning.

Before confronting him I tried to rationalize my actions. First, I told myself, I would point out that the French were our allies, and what are allies for? No, that was banal and stupid. But wasn't it true that the French occupation zone had been carved out of the American one, partially to assuage French pride but also to give them a share in the occupation duties in Germany? Irrelevant, I concluded; after all, a zone is a zone, and there is to be no transfer of DPs between them, period. As I pondered these justifications, a vision flitted across my mind: the sneering, threatening indignation of the Sixty-third Division commander, who would have eagerly had me court-martialed if it had not been for Colonel Winning. And this is how I thanked him—with more insubordination?

Also, the nagging thought that military regulations were made for good, solid reasons and it usually made no sense to violate them, regardless of one's strong, personal feelings, kept returning to my mind. The fact was, I had disregarded the rules. For all I knew, the Radom Jews could have been picked up by some other military government official and perhaps handled in a better fashion. Of course, no one knew if that would have happened, not at that particular time, but I wondered what the colonel's conclusion would be.

"From Radom, Poland, you say." Winning carefully regarded me as I stood before him in his office.

"Yes sir. Madam Vaison brought them over from the French zone in our trucks. She went with us to settle them in and get things set up."

"What do you know about them?"

"Only that there's just a few of them left—all men; the women and children were separated long ago. When Weiss and I saw them at Neuenberg, they poured their hearts out to us." I then explained as much as I knew at the time about the story of the Radom Jews, based upon the accounts Guttman and others had given me. Winning listened in rapt attention. "The Germans left them to die of typhus and starvation at Vaihingen when the French came to liberate them in April," I concluded. "They've been in the French zone since."

"How did you settle on Bensheim?"

"It was the only place we could find. It's an old schoolhouse that we made over." I paused for a moment. "They're rather more comfortable, I think. Their health's improving."

He smiled. "I suppose the chaplain gave, shall we say, his blessing to this operation."

Blessing? He instigated it.

"Lieutenant?"

Maybe he did, but I was still the guy in charge.

I swallowed hard. "Colonel, I take full responsibility for these actions, and ..."

He waved me silent. "I know you do, Al." He grinned. "Frankly, I would have thought less of you if you hadn't tried to help them out. Don't worry, I'll smooth things over. The French owe us a lot."

My insides returned to their normal state.

"So we now have a Jewish DP camp," Winning continued, "to add to the rest of our most distinguished United Nations' roster of peoples." Again, with his smiling, engaging temperament, "I should like to visit them."

And so he did, on that same day, in fact. When our conversation ended, we hopped into his Mercedes Benz sports roadster parked outside and traveled the twenty miles to Bensheim. As it turned out, he was just the first among many of the "higher brass" to visit the Radom Jews.

With that problem behind me, we were soon faced with another, more serious one. More Jews were joining the Bensheim camp daily, arriving from the Seventh Army jurisdiction as well as from other areas, and we could expect the camp's population roughly to double by the end of the year. The old schoolhouse was fine for the present, but we had to look for more spacious quarters. Michel made an improbable suggestion.

"How about Heidelberg?" he asked.

"Heidelberg?"

"Of course. It's not terribly far from here, and the area is blanketed by huge estates, castles and everything. Why don't we take a trip and see?"

I was not about to dismiss a chance to drive around Heidelberg, particularly for officially sanctioned reasons. "It can't hurt to look, I suppose."

"Good, let's do it." And off we went.

Heidelberg is one of the most beautiful and famous cities in Germany. It also was one of the few that had fortunately escaped the wholesale destruction from Allied bombers that had leveled so many other urban centers in the country. Our daily routines had been glutted with scenes of destruction, and I was eager for a change.

Rich in historical significance and architectural splendor, Heidelberg possessed a world-renowned university and many magnificent buildings that were constructed during the German Renaissance. Among the most elaborate and gorgeous monuments in Heidelberg is its ancient *Schloss,* or castle. The *Schloss* is situated some three hundred feet above the Neckar River, along which run the most picturesque elements of the city. Although much of the structure was devastated during the religious wars of the sixteenth and seventeenth centuries, the *Schloss* still endows its visitors with a magnificent, panoramic view of the area. Indeed, the majesty of the city's ancient cathedrals and the quaint, compelling charm of the medieval houses located along the *Haupstrasse*, the street running parallel to the Neckar River, are visible from the site of the *Schloss*. I was hoping that I could escape for another chance to wander around the city and take in the sights.

As it turned out, I didn't, but traveling through the area surrounding that enchanting city was equally worthwhile. Our trip took us on winding roads through the lavishly wooded area around Heidelberg, abundantly endowed with vineyards and large, landed estates. We ended up in the village of Langenzelle, about ten miles from Heidelberg, inspecting the facilities of *Schloss Langenzelle,* a beautiful and spacious castle owned by a German countess. She was not in residence at the time. Michel and I walked through the *Schloss* to find it inhabited by a mixture of Germans, Ukrainians, and Latvians, and it was not clear who actually was in charge. We had to find this out, of course, and then obtain the authority to commandeer the building and direct evictions of its present inhabitants—all rather unpleasant tasks.

The structure itself was excellent. Although in slight disrepair and badly in need of a thorough scrubbing, this German castle presented a picture of breath-taking beauty. Its quoin corners led up to elaborately decorated gables that extended beyond the pitch of the roof, highlighting the castle's comely, exterior dimensions. The gables' majestic lines were only slightly overshadowed by rectangular towers peaked with conical turrets located in the background at each end of the building. All this coronated a ten-acre setting rich in foliage, spacious fields, a pond with rowboats, vegetable gardens, and winding paths fragrantly colored with flowers.

The interior was equally impressive and particularly appropriate for the functions of a normal family life. The castle contained many small bedrooms and several very large ones. A spacious dining hall complemented an even larger multipurpose room, where group activities could take place. The sanitary facilities remained intact, although insufficient for the number of people we had in mind. All in all, however, one could hardly ask for a better solution to our space problem—an ancient German castle.

After walking through the premises and informing its present inhabitants that we intended to requisition the building for use by the American Military Government, Michel and I returned to the jeep and exchanged looks of satisfaction.

"Perfect," he declared.

I agreed, but said, "Well, it has to be cleaned up."

"That's right, Lieutenant," Michel replied. Then this veteran of eleven concentration camps smiled at me with a casual, disingenuous hauteur and remarked, "If there's one thing I can't stand, it's a dirty castle."

Off we drove back to Mannheim and Bensheim to my "Big Jewish Family," to prepare them for the last leg of their journey from a death camp to a castle.

Of course, *Schloss Langenzelle* was not the last stop for the Radom Jews before they went their separate ways, although it was a very important one and certainly the most memorable for its symbolic impact. Yet, for all its grandeur, that old castle was still a Displaced Persons Camp. Although it was one of the smaller ones under my jurisdiction, I constantly fretted about it, even though its residents managed their own affairs competently with little need for outside intervention. I worried about what was going to happen to them, what country would take them, where they would end up, and how they would get there. The majority of the DPs our unit received and shipped out all had homes to go to. Their journeys ended triumphantly; their stories had happy endings.

Other groups had different destinies. The future was always uncertain for the Jews.

And, then, there were the Ukrainians …

Lt. Albert A. Hutler, Mannheim, Germany, 1945

Ernest Michel's 60th birthday, photo taken in front of Auschwitz concentration camp

Convoy of Belgium DPs returned to Brussels, April 5, 1945

Sending the DPs home to France, 1945

Chapter Four

Back to Hell: The Soviet DPs

Visitors: Soviets and Ukrainians

The Soviet officer towered over the young woman, intimidating her with his height, his bearing. Rigid and unsmiling, he displayed a visage that defied the most astute memory to recall five minutes after his welcome departure. With cold eyes, an expressionless mouth, and a face that relinquished no intimation of any thoughts unrelated to his profession, the soldier virtually trumpeted his presence before the fearful Ukrainians. He and his companion exuded a subdued truculence that filled the room with tension.

Soviet uniforms were impressive, however, and suffused their bodies with a chilly dignity. Their drab brown attire was buttoned up to the collar, which was wrapped tightly around the neck in the fashion of an American marine's dress uniform or a chaplain's collar. Gold-colored epaulets highlighted their shoulders and red bands circled the sleeves on their left arms just above the elbow. Their hats, the Soviet version of the American army flat cap, looked like the miniature hull of an overturned ship; a red star decorated its center where two seams met at the front. The soldiers' chests were garnished with full dress ribbons and hanging medal pendants filled with minute designs. Someone once told me that Soviet troops were known to favor decorations over helmets—not just on parade, but in *combat*. Perhaps this made sense; when I accompanied him through the section of Kaiser Wilhelm Kaserne reserved for Baltics and Ukrainians, I sometimes felt as though we *were* in combat.

"Your name?" he snapped.

The question was interpreted for me by the elected chairman of the group. He was a Ukrainian.

"Sonya Stepstyevsky," she replied.

"Age?"

"Eighteen."

"Your family, how many people in it?"

"Seven. That's my parents, me, two brothers, two sisters."

"How long did your family live in Soviet Union?"

The answer stuttered on her lips; a pause followed.

"We lived in Ukraine all our lives. We ..."

"You lived in Soviet Union! Now answer me, how long? How many years? How did you get here in Germany?" He glowered at her.

"May I remind you, sir," I said, addressing the officer, "that your responsibility is to obtain information about the person, not to argue with anyone or to threaten them."

His contemptuous stare moved slowly in my direction, like the cannon on a tank turret adjusting its sight, focusing on a new target. But he said nothing.

He didn't have to. The Soviets could claim these people as they pleased, and they knew it. Seventh Army directives indicated that Ukrainians, Baltic peoples, and Poles from areas east of the Curzon Line could not be forced to return to their country of origin unless they were designated as being Soviet citizens by a Soviet officer.[1] Thus, in practice, these DPs had no choice about returning to their native lands—which made them unique among all the other nationalities. Further, Soviet officers had immediate access to DP camps in our zone, along with the right to question all those in sections reserved for Soviet nationalities. They had to be accompanied by an American officer—that was my job—but they held the fate of these people in their hands. And there was nothing we could do about it.

"How is it you are here, in this zone of occupation?" he continued.

---

[1]The Curzon Line was a boundary established between Poland and the USSR in 1939. Polish boundaries prior to that date were farther east, and when the new boundary was established, many Poles ended up in Soviet territory. Hence, they became without their knowledge or consent, Soviet citizens.

"We were taken here by the Germans to work in a factory. When the Americans came, they liberated us, and we ended up here." She emphasized the word "liberated." The Soviet sneered at her.

"Did you collaborate with the Germans?"

"No!"

He gave her a look that showed he did not believe her. His expression, icy and contemptuous, issued forth power, total power. It didn't matter whether or not he believed her; he controlled what happened to her and to all the others in this section of the camp. Accompanying Soviet authorities as they went through our DP camps, arbitrarily picking out their "citizens" among the mixture of nationalities, had all the dignity of culling chickens in a barnyard. The process sometimes made *me* feel like a collaborator.

The term "collaborator" was odious to this Soviet officer, however; and for good reason. When the Germans swept into the western part of the Soviet Union during their invasion of 1941, they were greeted by non-Russian minorities who threw flowers in the paths of panzer tanks. The brutality of Stalin's rule had convinced them that the Germans were liberators. Indeed, postwar studies confirmed that at least one million troops fighting for the Germans on the Russian front were drawn from these groups. When the Germans retreated, these recruited minorities, along with many Russians who had fought against the Red Army, went with them. Many thousands ended up in Western DP camps.

Stalin regarded all those who had fought with the Germans as traitors . But many in the Western DP camps had been in German POW camps or had been scooped up by

German armies and shipped back to the Reich to work in factories. But these circumstances made no difference to the Soviet dictator. Stalin ordered their repatriation anyway, in order to punish all those who had had any contact with the Germans, regardless of the reasons. It is true that many Ukrainians and others had been "collaborators" in that they had joined the Germans' horrible persecution of minorities, including Jews. Most, however, simply desired to be free of Soviet communism. Our experience in the Seventh Army area indicated that non-Russian minorities, as well as many Russians, would do anything, including commit suicide, to avoid facing the wrath of Soviet authorities.

It should be added that most ethnic Russians were glad to return to the Soviet Union. For them a Soviet soldier questioning their backgrounds presented no problem; they were used to such things. In fact, Russian nationals were often pleased to see Soviet authorities and greeted their arrival with songs and tears. Since early June, we had moved some thirty thousand Russian nationals through our area to Soviet repatriation camps, after which they were transported by rail to the Soviet Union. They were as anxious to leave Germany as we were eager to send them on their way.

But the people before us now were not Russian nationals. They were Ukrainians, Poles, Lithuanians, Latvians, and Estonians.

"You are a citizen of the Soviet Union," he announced. "You will return."

She began to cry. A man standing close to her began to protest vigorously. Their objections only made the Soviet officer angrier, and he questioned the others in an even more brusque, threatening manner. The questions spat out: name, age, family, where are you from, how long were you there, how did you get into German hands, what did you do for the Germans, how did you get here at this camp, how long have you been here? And they always terminated with the conclusion, abrupt, final, terrifying, like a death sentence: "You are a Soviet citizen and will be returned to the Soviet Union." It was a heart-rending process.

The Soviet soldier concluded his questioning, looked at me, and signaled our exit from the camp. We turned toward the door, passing rows of double beds beside which stood the Ukrainians. He walked before me. Our departure was accompanied by baleful stares, which seemed almost physically perceptible, like waves of tension against the back of my neck, throbbing, pushing me out of the door. In their eyes, I was an accomplice. In the courtyard, the Soviets saluted smartly and were off. I knew I would see them again soon.

The following morning, sitting behind my desk, I could hear footsteps approaching my office.

"There is someone here to see you, Lieutenant," a voice called out. I looked up from the papers on my desk to confront the distinguished bearing of Kal Plessner, a second lieutenant on my staff. Plessner's gray hair, erect posture, and authoritative gait made him look more like a general than a junior grade officer. I once told him he probably was the oldest second lieutenant in the army, a charge that bothered him not a bit. With smiling eyes that warmed his face and made those around him feel comfortable, he exuded the confidence, charm, and poise that suited him perfectly to his job—commanding Kaiser Wilhelm Kaserne. He was also gifted with a ready wit that often defused tense situations we frequently had to deal with at the office. As it turned out, on that day, August 30, I would need every measure of help he could provide.

"Who is it?" I asked.

"The Soviet representative," Plessner nodded his head and darted his eyes to one side, indicating they were within earshot, "and his interpreter."

This was sooner than I thought. I groaned inwardly.

"Let them in."

The two men I was with the day before quickly strode into my office and presented themselves, stiffly. Their authoritative primness led me to speculate about how they appeared during their casual moments. I wondered if they *had* any casual moments.

The senior officer bore his dark eyes into me. Not today, I thought.

"Lieutenant," he greeted me formally. This was translated.

"Captain," I returned.

"As you know, the designation process is complete, Lieutenant. I therefore request your assistance to move Soviet citizens from the Kaiser Wilhelm Kaserne camp. We'll need trucks and military assistance to maintain order." Then, loosening up a bit, "nothing out of the ordinary, you know. These are among the last, and we want to move them out and back home and close things up. They'll be moved to our camp in Heidelberg."

To the Soviet camp, I thought, deep in the American occupation zone. I had always thought that the Western Allies went to unnecessary lengths to appease Soviet sensibilities in the repatriation process, particularly in allowing them to operate their own DP camps in Western zones. The Soviets administered their areas sternly, using their familiar methods—strict, sometimes brutal, authoritarian control. Soviet commanders dictated the camps' command hierarchy and legal-administrative structure. In short, they were more like POW camps than temporary quarters for the displaced.

Soviet camps had presented enormous problems for AMG authorities. Their DPs, Russian and non-Russian minorities alike, evinced more unbridled hatred toward the Germans than any other group under our jurisdiction. They took every opportunity to ravage the German population—looting, muggings, rape, robbery, assault—their vengeance had no limits. Further, they were well organized, armed, and heavily involved in black market operations, constituting a sort of temporary Mafia organized along nationality lines.

The extent of their criminal activity became evident when, acting on an informant's tip, a joint American-Soviet task force, in which I participated, raided the Heidelberg camp. The mission began at six in the morning. Soviet and American soldiers hustled the DPs, stumbling, half-awake, and barely dressed, out into the courtyard and carried out a thorough search of the premises. We rifled through everything—lockers, baggage, trunks, mattresses, pillows; soldiers even inspected the toilets. Our investigation uncovered a pirate's cache of stolen goods, indicating that the camp was the headquarters of a huge operation, especially in currency—American-issued occupation marks. The offenders were rounded up and dealt with by the Soviet authorities. I never did hear what happened to them.

"There are also more reports of anti-Soviet propaganda being passed along in the camp, Lieutenant," the captain continued sternly. "And we saw some of this yesterday. We shall not tolerate such things. Your directives order you to stop such activity."

His effrontery galled me. I didn't need to be informed about American military directives by a Soviet soldier. "They require me to 'investigate' it," I corrected.

He ignored that qualification. "Attempts to persuade Soviet citizens to refuse repatriation is a crime, Lieutenant. All Soviet citizens desire to return to the motherland."

The hell they do, I thought. Russians, probably; but not Lithuanians, Estonians, Latvians, or Poles. And certainly not Ukrainians.

"It is only the collaborationists who resist. We know how to deal with them."

"I'm sure you do," I eyed him coolly. "When shall we transport them?"

"On the sixth."

"Very well. We'll be in contact." We saluted each other, and the two Russians left.

I leaned back in my chair and sighed heavily. Looking in the direction of the departing Russians, Plessner turned the corners of his mouth down with an affected expression of cowering obeisance. Sergeant Weiss entered the room just as Plessner asked me one of his less profound questions:

"Who are the bad guys again, Al? I forget."

I gave him a humorless smile. "There weren't supposed to be any more after V-E Day."

Weiss looked perplexed. "What was that all about?" he asked.

"The Ukrainians," I answered.

Weiss had seen as much resistance among the eastern European DPs as I had; more, in fact.

"This doesn't fall under the category of 'mitzvah'," he observed.

"Only if we could prevent their going," Plessner said.

Turning to him, I asked, "How many Ukrainians are at your camp?"

"About six hundred fifty."

"And how many do you think want to go back?"

"None—or maybe a few. But not many."

"A lot of them will probably desert," Weiss said. "Every camp in our area where the Russians have come has had that experience. The last thing you want to do is to tell them that they're going back to Russia."

Plessner rubbed his chin thoughtfully. "We're going to lose at least two-thirds of them if they find out, Al. They would all go if they had the means."

"Then I guess we just can't tell them," I said.

Weiss looked at me with a how-can-we-do-this expression that made me feel horrible. But we knew we had no choice.

"Our orders haven't changed, gentlemen. We're going to carry them out and transport the Ukrainians on the sixth, as planned." I looked at Sergeant Weiss and said, "We'll need at least ten trucks."

"I'll get them."

"Kal, do your best to keep things quiet."

He nodded his assent.

"And I'll get the troops to watch over the transfer."

We fixed our eyes on one another briefly, with the silent dread that comes from sharing a mutual distaste for following unpleasant orders. With these instructions, the meeting ended, and I turned my attention to other matters.

Three days later, I was visited by an impromptu delegation of Ukrainians who claimed to represent three thousand DPs from Kaiser Wilhelm Kaserne. Weiss led them in and stayed with me to hear their entreaties and help translate.

It was a pitiful, depressing scene: Weiss, myself, and the hastily convened "committee" of Ukrainians, with haggard, sorrowful countenances. Patiently, through an interpreter, I listened to their case.

"We heard that Soviet repatriation officers are taking us back to Soviet Union," a spokesman said.

"Yes, that is true. You are scheduled to leave on the sixth for the Soviet camp at Heidelberg."

"We cannot go back to Soviet Union. You must stop this."

"I cannot stop the movement of Soviet citizens by Soviet authorities," I explained officiously. "The Ukraine is not considered a separate country by the Allied governments. It is part of the Soviet Union. You are regarded as Soviet citizens. Therefore, you must return to the Soviet Union."

"We are Ukrainians." The pitch of his voice raised.

"The Ukraine is considered part of the Soviet Union," I repeated, recognizing that this was a political statement that would not make any sense to this delegation in terms of national loyalties.

"If we go back to the Ukraine, we will go to labor camps. We will be shot. It is like ordering our execution."

"Why? Were you guilty of any crimes?" Some of these Ukrainians may have been collaborationists. My question allowed me to shift the direction of his remarks.

But the suggestion of wrongdoing only served to inflame them, and they greeted it with a buzzing, angry murmur. Another stepped forward, pushing aside the first spokesman. His words issued forth in angry spurts, and the translator had a difficult time keeping up.

"You do not have to be guilty of crime to be arrested in Soviet Union!" he shouted, towering over my desk.

I felt an onslaught coming on.

"In Ukraine in 1930," he continued amid agreeing nods and gestures among his friends, "in 1931, in 1932, there is no food. There is famine, and people starve to death. The police come, the army, OGPU,[1] they come, they take everything. People are divided into groups." He put his whole body into the explanation, moving it this way and that, waving his arms in wide sweeps up, down, and sideways. "There is this group, there is that group, and there is that group. This group stays, this group goes and no one sees them again, and this group ..." he paused, "is shot." Running his hand across his mouth to wipe away the moisture and regain his composure, the spokesman continued his story. His friends participated avidly with increasingly vocal expressions of agreement.

---

[1]Obedinennoe Gosudarstvennoe Politicheskoe Upravlenye—Unified State Political Administration, the name of the Soviet secret police during the 1930s and the forerunner to the KGB.

"The OGPU man comes up to me and pushes me down. He takes his gun. Like this, see?" Again he acts out the scene. "And he says to get out. And he takes gun and butts me with it and takes everything out of my house, everything we own. Now I have nothing. I have no cattle. OGPU take the cattle, the house, the food, even our clothes, and now I have nothing. My family, my wife, my sons, my mother—we go to *kolkhoz.*[1] Nobody wants to go. They force us to go to live on big farm. They march us off with their guns pointed at us to live on the *kolkhoz.*" He paused. "A big farm where we have no money, no cattle, no food—where we starve."

Another stepped forward, speaking slowly. "I know many *kulaks*[2] who killed themselves. A man kills his wife, his children, then he kills himself." His slow, careful delivery hushed the murmurs. "It was the best thing," he concluded.

"On the roads," another continued. "I saw dead bodies, dead *kulaks* on the roads. They run away and die. OGPU drives them out, and they have no place to go, so they walk away on the roads and lay down and die. A wagon comes by and picks them up. I made it all the way. I made it to the city," he said with some pride. "Eventually I got bread."

"Bread!" someone exclaimed. "We made bread from weeds. This bread from this weed, that bread from that weed. Porridge from another weed, with sawdust, and tree bark."

I had no response to these stories. Aimlessly, I asked, "When did you have to do that?"

---

[1]A Soviet collective farm.

[2]The better off peasants whom Stalin was determined to destroy. He succeeded.

Several looked at each other. "1932," came one response. "Yes, 1933, also. The worst was over in 1935, I think. All we did was to survive in those years, through famine and the purges."

A voice from the back muttered, "Then the Germans came."

No one turned to acknowledge or to elaborate on this remark. The phrase spoke hugely for the events that followed, and to explain it would amount to self-incrimination. The Ukrainians thought the Nazis would free them. I wondered how many of this group had joined the Germans without partaking in their persecutions.

"I must again inform you that my hands are tied, and I have no choice in the matter," I said, trying to conclude the meeting. "I'm under orders to have you shipped to the Soviet repatriation camp."

I'm under orders, I have no choice; where have I heard this excuse before?

"There's nothing else I can do. I'm sorry."

There was a deadly pause as the group slowly digested my words. Slowly they filed out of my office, despondent, angry, and without hope. September sixth loomed before us ominously.

Confrontations

On the morning of September 6, 1945, ten deuce-and-a-half trucks—army slang for trucks with two sets of doubled rear wheels—lumbered into Kaiser Wilhelm Kaserne. They were manned by American soldiers of Puerto Rican extraction, many of whom could barely speak English, much less German. A captain commanded them. They were among the huge contingent of replacements sent to Germany for occupation duty after the war. I always thought that letting the veterans go in such large numbers was a mistake; they knew the country, the people, and their problems much better than these ill-prepared troops. And by the time the new soldiers learned what they needed to know to become effective administrators, their tour of duty was up.

The trucks, dusty green hulks with harsh, rectangular contours, lined up before the embarkation point. Their tail pipes belched out exhaust fumes that fouled the crisp morning air. Rumbling diesel engines crowded out other sounds as they intermittently revved up, beckoning ominously amidst stares of dread from the onlookers. Plessner, Weiss, and I stood near a truck, listening to the grating, tinny squawk of the loudspeakers bellowing out orders in Ukrainian.

"Attention! Attention! Report to the trucks for embarkation! Repeat! Report to the trucks for embarkation! Take your belongings with you! Register for embarkation at the trucks! Attention! Attention! ..."

A solitary figure meekly approached the first truck. He was followed by another. They shot baneful looks in our direction. Others did not follow them, however. The Ukrainians were not coming; they stayed in the barracks or huddled close to the building, glaring at the American troops.

We scanned the grounds anxiously—trucks, barracks, windows, fences. The atmosphere was electric with anticipation, and the troops exchanged skittish glances, first at the captain, then at me, seeking direction. Hundreds of other DPs watched in an area cordoned off from the Ukrainian section. They, too, wondered what the Americans were going to do.

The captain of the truck brigade signaled to a squad of troops to approach the stubborn DPs. I approached with them. Waving their arms with angry, impatient gestures, a few soldiers shouted at the Ukrainians closest to them and the trucks. Some of them waved their rifles in sweeping motions, urging them to get onto the trucks. Finally, a GI grabbed a young man by the scruff of the neck and dragged him toward the truck, against the protests of his mother. Other soldiers followed suit, pushing, shoving, and talking in a language no one understood.

Children shrieked, men shouted, women howled and pleaded with the American soldiers not to stuff them onto the trucks. Individuals of all ages fell to their knees wailing and begging us, *begging us,* not to take them away.

A scream sailed across the air, above the mob. I looked toward the barracks. On the third floor, a mother crouched herself in an open window, grasping a child. Behind her but only partially visible from my vantage point was an American soldier. I could see his shadowy figure motioning to the woman, the muzzle of his M-1 glinting sporadically in the sunlight as he grunted commands for her to go with him. She stayed put.

In desperation, several Ukrainian men ripped open their shirts and bared their chests, shouting, "Shoot me now! Kill me! I'm dead if I go back to Russia anyway. Do it now! Get it over with!" But the only shots that were fired went into the air, as we attempted to quiet the mob down.

The other DPs standing behind the fenced-off partitions viewed the scene in sullen shock, astonished at the sight of American soldiers carrying out acts that only Germans, they thought, were capable of perpetrating.

"Fascists!" someone spat out.

This dumbfounded me.

"Que?" one of the GIs asked.

"Good Lord! Did you hear what they called us?" another said.

"Who do they think we are?"

An answer came quickly from a dark-haired GI standing by a truck. "They think we're Krauts, Nazis! What do you think they think?"

"They know we're not Germans!"

"Tell them that."

The adolescent voice of a young soldier emitted from the cab of a deuce-and-a-half near me, its baritone pitch separating it from the others. "Holy Mother! Are we really supposed to be doing this?"

The hubbub swallowed the question.

"Come on, lady, come on!" A soldier dragged a whimpering, pleading woman across the dirt, grabbing her clothing by the neck and shoulder, like a gunny sack. A small child grasped her mother's ankles, crying, while another, an older boy, hobbled beside them—a train of individuals clawing, scrapping the earth, leaving their marks on the ground, under the awkward, unsure prodding of a soldier. Onto the truck they went.

A child jumped off the back of a vehicle, caught his clothing on a sharp angle, scraped an arm, cracked his head against the bumper, and tumbled to the ground, bloodied and screaming. A soldier approached and helped him up. The GI pulled, pushed, then finally grabbed and heaved the light body aboard. It landed with a thud and a howl of pain. Instantly the soldier bounded onto the truck's flatbed, cursed, looked at the crying passengers, and uttered an apology. Irrelevant, absurd. Off he went to get another.

A tangle of figures across the yard, DPs and Americans, caught my eye. Arms and legs flailed against grasping, pulling hands: an elbow in the back, the ribs, the side of a head; knees and feet, springing, jerking, jabbing into bodies; tearing clothes, crying, swearing, threatening; a random kick in the groin; vomiting, writhing in the dirt; a raised fist, the butt of a rifle high in the air, cocked, ready to strike …

"Hold it!"

No effect..

"Hold it! Stop! Hold it right there!"

Heads turned toward my voice, slowly.

"Put it down! Now! Leave him alone: let him go! Get away from there! Let her be! Stop!"

I marched around the yard snapping orders to this group and that, breaking up scuffles, ordering weapons lowered and tempers cooled. "That's enough, no more, we're done."

"Sir?"

"That's it, we're done, no more today. Let go."

"My orders …"

"I'm giving you new ones. Captain!"

Orders shouted out—mine and the captain's. The mob quieted; shouts simmered to murmurs and then to silence. The captain of the convoy came up to me.

He was agitated, angry. "I don't like this any better than you, Lieutenant, but my orders are to ship them to Heidelberg. I can't leave them here. They'll have my ass!"

"Thanks for your help, for getting things quiet, Captain."

"Sure, fine, but I still gotta move 'em out."

"Not today, not this way."

"Well then, when?"

"Maybe not at all, I hope. I want to talk to them."

"I don't know what difference that will make. We still have to truck 'em out."

"Look, I'll take full responsibility. They're under my jurisdiction in this camp, anyway. Just move your men out. We can't ship these people out like this. It's madness."

"All right," he said.

The captain turned and motioned to his troops to gather by the trucks. Quickly they boarded the vehicles, and the convoy rumbled off.

I was left with several hundred confused Ukrainians and a worried, disgruntled staff.

"Now what do we do?" Plessner asked. "We still have to move them out." The DPs were dispersing and heading into the building.

"I want to have an outdoor meeting with them," I said. "We've got to get some things straight. Don't let them go back to the barracks until I talk with them."

"Right." Plessner was finally able to restore order. Acting like a cross between a shepherd corralling wayward sheep and a first sergeant barking out commands, he gathered the Ukrainians before me.

I looked at them, studied their faces. They were still distraught and uncertain, though many showed relief. All returned my gaze with expectant, wondering looks. With an interpreter at my side and my hands on my hips, I sighed, took a deep breath, and began:

"Now listen to me. This has got to stop, you've got to go. I'll talk with my superiors and ask that American troops and trucks don't come the next time. No American troops, no trucks. OK? And I'll get back to you. But you must prepare yourselves."

I repeated this line until they seemed to calm down, then dismissed them. I walked slowly back to my jeep as images of my initial encounter with the Radom Jews flitted across my mind. That had been the first time a group of desperate people had looked at me as though I were God. Miraculously, I was able to help them, temporarily at least.

But this time, in spite of my words, I felt helpless.

The Aftermath

By the end of September 1945, my American Military Government unit had shipped over a quarter million DPs back to their homelands. In the wake of their homecomings came reports of Frenchmen bolting out of trucks and trains to kiss the ground of France; of Hollanders dancing and singing in the streets of Amsterdam; of Belgians tearfully rejoicing in Liege and Brussels; and of Greeks kissing and embracing the hulks of the British transport planes that had taken them home to their native land. Even the Russians were known to paint pictures of Stalin at train depots on their way back to Mother Russia. Tales of wrenching voyages culminating in ecstatic homecomings filtered back to us in Mannheim, giving us the quiet satisfaction we often needed to keep up our morale during those hectic days.

But what about the Ukrainians?

With numerous memos and requests I tried to get SHAEF officials to change their policy about Americans assistance in the shipment of Soviet DPs. Surprisingly, our orders were changed, rather quickly, in fact. Shortly after September 6, the policy stipulated that all persons designated as Soviet citizens be transported by Soviet troops using Soviet trucks. Finally, on September 13, less than four hundred Ukrainians out of the original 650 were moved without incident by the Russians from Kaiser Wilhelm Kaserne to the Soviet DP camp in Heidelberg. I never heard from that group again. They disappeared, without a trace, into the black hole of the Soviet Union.

Years after the war, scholars were able to unearth what happened to most returnees to the Soviet Union. In their magisterial review of Soviet history, Mikhail Heller and Aleksandr M. Nekrich report that nearly all Soviet prisoners of war (note that they were classified as POWs, not just DPs) were regarded as traitors and dealt with accordingly.[1] All

---

[1]Mikhail Heller and Aleksandr M. Nekrich, *Utopia in Power: The History of the Soviet Union from 1917 to the Present*, trans. Phyllis B. Carlos (New York: Summit Books, 1986), pp. 45-56.

were considered guilty, and no one was tried individually; they were reviewed in groups and sentenced by special three-man boards. One-fifth was sentenced to death or given twenty-five years hard labor in the infamous Soviet labor camps. Indeed, in the ports of Murmansk and Odessa, British sailors reported that Soviet secret police *shot the returnees on the docks,* in full sight of British officers and men.

Another fifteen to twenty percent of the POWs and similarly designated individuals were sentenced to five to ten years hard labor; ten percent were sent into exile in Siberia; and fifteen percent went to labor brigades to rebuild areas ravaged by the war. Of the remainder, only about half returned to their homes, and the rest died en route to the Soviet Union, escaped, were shot, or were somehow unaccounted for. Such was the destiny of Soviet "citizens"—most of them loyal soldiers—who fell into the hands of Russian authorities after the war.

Chapter Five

Changing the Guardians

Confronting the Radomers

"Yes, it has been beautiful," the man responded. "So different, so unexpected. In some ways, I don't want it ever to end. But I know that some day it must. I want to go home, but I just don't know where home is. Not yet."

I nodded in agreement, appreciating his honesty yet painfully aware of his predicament. The gorgeous setting of *Schloss Langenzelle* offered soothing, healing balms to these victims of the Holocaust, wounded in body and spirit. Their survival was a miracle, their recovery, a joy, a lift to one's faith in God and man. But "my Jews" could not stay at the castle indefinitely. They had to go sometime, and in the near future, too. The population at the castle had been increasing steadily since its opening in mid-June. Word of its existence among Jewish survivors had spread quickly. The thought that there was a haven for them run by a Jewish lieutenant (Kal Plessner), and a Canadian Jew, Miss Ethel Ostry, who worked for the United Nations Relief and Rehabilitation Administration (UNRRA), under the overall supervision of an American Jewish officer in charge of the DP section, was a powerful lure. My big Jewish family grew on a daily basis.

Our castle population increased for other reasons as well, often unpleasant and shameful. Frightening accounts of the treatment of Jewish DPs in other areas, especially those under General George Patton's command, had begun to circulate throughout the American zone. Patton was a brilliant general, but he was callous and insensitive about the problems of DPs. General Eisenhower had ordered that Jewish DPs be given special treatment and not be forced to return to their former countries of residence, but Patton and his officers ignored such directives. Repatriation "horror stories" filtered out. I had heard of some six hundred Polish Jews from his district who Patton had forced to return to Poland, in spite of their vehement protests. No news about what happened to them ever escaped Soviet-occupied Poland. I had seen enough such cases—Polish Jews, eastern European Jews, Russian minorities—and they made me shudder. No wonder Jewish survivors flocked to Langenzelle. No wonder that many American soldiers, after hearing their stories, showered them with attention, gifts, and other expressions of compassion and concern over their plight.

"Look, look over there," the camp resident said.

I turned my head toward the direction indicated by his eyes. Walking on the path to the castle were American GIs, officers and men, carrying gifts for the Jews of Radom and their families: clothing, cigars and cigarettes, tobacco, candy bars and chocolate, liquor, sweet cakes, sometimes their own rations. With each offering came rewards: looks of radiant gratitude, shimmering eyes, creased, smiling faces, bony arms gently embracing beefy GI torsos. The soldiers offered their greetings, left their gifts, and departed, their softly curled fists with fat, awkward fingers catching the wayward moisture on their faces.

Gallant men they were; courageous warriors, noble, brave, honest, not afraid to cry; volunteers on missions of mercy, having taken their own journeys through the hell of combat and the shock of liberating death camps, to succor the returnees from a worse hell. Wise men bearing gifts, I thought; heroes all. I loved them.

My God. What will happen when they leave? What will happen to the Jews?

"Lots of visitors," my companion said, smiling.

"And there are others to come, many, in fact," I replied. Should I bring up my reason for visiting the castle today? Disturb the moment? Add disagreement, strife?

"Yes, it is a pleasure to see … ," I continued, aimlessly. My statement had no impact. The man was looking beyond me, through me, as though I were not there.

I tried to pursue the thought. "I especially appreciate the officers … , um …" What was he looking at?

My companion had stopped breathing. His face turned pale; his mouth opened, gaping; his eyes widened, slowly getting bigger, pushing outward, it seemed. His whole face became longer, stretched, wet with perspiration and frozen in speechless astonishment.

He rushed past me and scampered furiously toward the road where a figure was running wildly to greet him. The two nearly crashed into each other, embracing, kissing, crying, tumbling over and enveloping each others' bodies.

A mother? No. A sister? Probably not. No, more likely his wife. Yes, that was it, his wife. It had to be his wife.

I watched them bubbling with joy. His earlier words drifted into my thoughts, now warm, content: "Lots of visitors," he had said. Yes, lots of them. And lots of surprises too.

"You must meet Lieutenant Hutler. This is Lieutenant Hutler," he sputtered in front of me. I tried to remain at a parade rest stance, stiff and awkward on that beautiful Saturday afternoon in the yard of the castle, hoping it would keep my composure. I listened to her remarkable tale.

It was his wife, all right. Her story tumbled out in spurts. Each had assumed the other was dead, but the wife, purely by accident, had seen his name and possible location in the Jewish DPs Central Committee's newspaper. She then proceeded, with a pack on her back, to traverse the length of Germany, walking and hitching rides from American army truck drivers until, five days later, she arrived at the village of Langenzelle. I happened to be there at the end of her quest, to witness their meeting. Like so many others, their reunion gushed with such a delirium of joy that the participants were left exhausted, spent.

The Central Committee of Jewish Survivors was responsible for many reunions like this, including that between Ernest and his sister, Lotte. She had reported her tale of survival in her letter to Ernest, the one he had read with such emotion in my office. Shortly after *Kristallnacht*, the Michels had decided to get Ernest and Lotte out of Germany as fast as they could. This was difficult: an affidavit, a visa, and a country of destination, few of which were willing to accept many Jews, were required. Ernest was too old to get classified as a child, but his parents were able to get Lotte on a children's transport to France. She was taken in by a Jewish family, where she stayed until her hosts were themselves carried off to a concentration camp.

They succeeded, however, in placing her in a convent, where she and other girls her age came under the care of Catholic nuns. In 1942 a heroic Swiss Jew used his own money along with funds supplied by the American Jewish Joint Distribution Committee to buy the children out of the convent, paying the Germans with United States dollars. With fifty other children, Lotte was shipped over the Pyrenees to Spain and from there to Palestine in safety. Like thousands of other Jews, she was saved by the nuns of France. Catholic nuns in other countries—Belgium, Italy, Holland—performed similar tasks of heroism.

"I'm happy for you both," I said to the newly reunited couple, as he vigorously shook my hand. I left them alone to continue with their rejoicing. I had other, less pleasant business to attend to. Sergeant Weiss, who had accompanied me on this trip, rejoined me from a distant corner of the yard. He came up to me smiling.

"Another reunion?"

I nodded. "The 'perks' part of our job."

He laughed. "The guests are thick today."

"I thought I saw you 'contribute' a few things yourself to the residents, Sergeant 'mitzvah.' "

"Well, just a few. Shouldn't we be talking to Guttman?" Weiss was conscientious to a fault; he never shirked anything. "How much are you going to discuss with him?" he asked. "Everything?"

"Well, one thing, at least. We still have a little time on the other."

"Not much," he replied, and we turned to walk toward the entrance.

We entered the castle and immediately encountered a young man who greeted us with a smile. I recognized him as one of the members of the camp council, a democratically elected body that governed the affairs of *Schloss Langenzelle*. I kept careful watch over the castle's residents and was familiar with all the members of its governing body.

Although the Radomers' setting was different from that of other DP camps, the governing structure was similar. Each camp—there were nine of them in my area—was run by an elected council and a chairman in conjunction with an AMG officer and several enlisted men. Together they formulated rules to guide the camp's operation and discussed the needs of the residents. Their concerns included everything associated with the conduct of a small community—medical needs, food and clothing, care for the aged and ill, social activities such as educational, cultural, and sports programs, and actions of the camp police. Nothing was outside their jurisdiction; even actions that took place outside the camp were dealt with, when appropriate.

Marek Guttman was the elected leader of the Langenzelle council, a position he had retained from when the

Radom Jews were in the French zone. Although physically recovered from his death camp days, he was still a pitiful, lean, sickly looking man. Guttman's frailties, however, were overshadowed by his striking visage—thick gray hair, deep-set, penetrating brown eyes, and a half smile that occupied his thin lips, permanent, ineradicable, triumphant over the years of misery and suffering. His mild demeanor issued a melancholy air, but that quickly evaporated when he spoke on matters of conviction, revealing the depth and strength of his character—a granite scarecrow, stolid, imperturbable. His determination to overcome tragedy, lift others up, and continue with his life symbolized the most courageous, noble, and tenacious attributes of the Radom Jews.

Guttman heard our voices and emerged from a room down the corridor to greet us. "How are you, Lieutenant?" he asked, his brilliant eyes keeping tune with his smiling lips. "Sergeant Weiss," he nodded.

"It's good to see you again, Marek," I replied, shaking his hand. "I would like to meet with you and the camp council." I shot some glances around the hallway. "There are some things that we should talk about."

Weiss managed a pale smirk.

"A mess, isn't it?" Guttman said. My displeasure with the condition of the castle was obvious.

"That's one of the things we must discuss. Colonel Winning plans a visit in a few days, and some, uh … preparations are in order."

This slightly formal tone evoked a quiet chuckle.

"Come with me," he said, and directed us into another room, away from the entrance to the building.

"Marek, this place is in horrible shape," I said, settling into an overstuffed chair. Weiss sat next to me, and Guttman placed his thin body on a chair next to a long table. He looked to me like a pencil-stick figure traced upon an erector set drawing; the background of the room protruded generously between the spaces formed by his slender, angular outline on the stiff, high-backed chair.

"Do you have any idea what kind of impression, *bad* impression, this place would make on the Colonel if he came by here now? This is a *castle*, for crying out loud, not a barracks. Jewish DPs have enough problems without handing your critics a ready-made excuse to sweep you under the rug, to send you someplace else, to shut the door and forget about you; which, not incidentally, is something else we're going to have to talk about, real soon."

"Yes, I agree," he replied evenly. "What do you propose we do?"

"About the castle? I propose you clean it up. What else?"

"How?"

A simple question, but exasperating. "Organize the residents into groups, get work brigades going … , you know. Pick it up; clean the place. There's junk all over. I think you should get some volunteers together and get on with it."

Guttman looked at me for a long moment. *"Volunteers?"* he asked.

"Yes, of course, volunteers. Get 'em all together. It shouldn't take too long if everyone pitches in."

Again silence. Finally, "No, Lieutenant, I'm not going to do that, and the council will not agree either. The grounds must be cleaned up, but the residents should not have to do it. Not after all we've been through. It's not our job."

"Well, whose job is it, then?"

"It's not our job," he said again, quietly.

This nonanswer was repeated, with variations, each time I emphasized the necessity to take action. Finally, I ran out of ways to make my point. Impatiently, I snapped, "Marek, as much as I think of you, I am going to have to *order* you and the council to prepare this camp for Colonel Winning's visit. As the American officer in charge, that is my duty."

Guttman showed no expression. Weiss shifted in his chair uneasily, giving me a pained look. He didn't like confrontations. I didn't either, but I still had a job to do.

"Further," I continued, imposing my most stiff military bearing, "I can, if necessary, deprive this camp of extra rations, chocolates, cigarettes, beer, and other amenities."

I paused, waiting for his reaction. None came.

"I can also order the substitution of powdered eggs and powdered milk for the fresh products you've been getting."

Still no reaction.

"I am prepared to take additional actions *if necessary,*" I concluded. The pitch of my last words scooped the air in a shrill, upward sweep, issuing forth a 'so-what-do-you-think-of-that' tone.

Guttman looked at me with sadness, his permanent smile flattened, his eyes, dark and heavy.

Finally he spoke, his commanding voice filling the room. "Lieutenant Hutler, you are our 'father.' We all love you and respect you very much. We all cherish what you mean to us and will never forget how you saved us." He paused, looking down, searching for words.

"For years," Guttman continued, "many years, we have been forced to clean the Germans' dirt." Marek fixed his eyes on me. There was steel in his words, in his gaze. "No more," he said. "No more, never, ever again."

He took a deep breath, signaling that there were more words to come, a conclusion.

"If you want *Schloss Langenzelle* to be clean for the visit of your Colonel, then get the Germans from the village to come in and do the cleaning. It is only just." Then he added, grimly, with words that stung, "What makes you think you can do more to us than Hitler did?"

His remark immobilized me, like a heavy weight pushing down on my thoughts, leaving me speechless, breathless. My lips parted slightly, but no words came out. A quick glance revealed that Weiss had turned his eyes on me also; he was on Guttman's side. The silence was audible.

Marek is absolutely right. Why should they *do it?*

A sound tripped into the room, a squeak, out of place but entirely welcome. I think it was Weiss, but it could have been me. We smiled at one another, then began to laugh softly, Weiss, Guttman, and myself. The tension in the room disappeared in an instant, and we were in communion with one another again. The confrontation between us was unnatural; it could not be sustained by something so flimsy as a recitation of my official duties. I could not win an argument with the likes of Guttman.

Weiss got up, gave me a grin, nodded to Guttman, and dashed out of the room, off the castle grounds, and toward the village to requisition the necessary help. I quickly wondered what the Burgermeister from Langenzelle would say. Better to give *him* an ultimatum, I thought; not Guttman.

I don't argue with Burgermeisters. But the iron wraith before me was invincible.

"Is there anything else?" he asked, with an engaging innocence. The smile resumed its rightful place; his dark eyes sparkled, sending forth playful twinkles of light from deep wells of resolve.

"No, I think that's all for today," I replied, with the air of a person who had gotten his way. Well, one thing at a time, I thought. First the visit of Colonel Winning, then the other business, the more frightening, serious problem we had to solve. I couldn't afford to lose two arguments in one day.

"Very fine, Lieutenant," Guttman said, getting up. "I'm sure the grounds will be in excellent shape for the Colonel's visit," he said, with the assurance of one who knew that *his* problem had now become *my* problem. No matter; it would be solved. But the more serious difficulty of what would happen to Radomers and other Jews in the camp as the castle population grew, forcing them all to leave, remained. And what about the replacements coming in to administer the camps, the repatriation process—green GIs from the States, UNRRA bureaucrats, busy, preoccupied officers? How would my big Jewish family and other displaced persons fare under such people? These things haunted my thoughts.

New Masters, Old Views

Marek and the camp council realized, as I did, that cleaning the castle was a trivial problem compared to the vastly more serious question of Jewish relocation. My own experience as a Jewish American citizen, horribly supplemented by the accounts of Jewish survivors in Europe, pointed to one conclusion: it didn't matter what Jews *did;* the fact that they were Jews was enough to condemn them. The legacy of anti-Semitism continued to burn in the embers of war-ravaged Europe. It flared among the human wreckage around us, spitting hatred into our faces. The air in occupied Germany remained poisoned, putrid; sometimes we choked.

I shall never forget a certain army major, a stiff, no-nonsense type who represented the wave of change for DP camp administration as the autumn months approached.

Bensheim, Germany—site of our Polish DP camp; formerly administered by a very competent army captain who himself was Polish; now administered by an American major. I traveled to Bensheim to visit him, hoping to convey our section's philosophy about the treatment of displaced persons and about coping with the special problems presented by survivors of the Holocaust. Colonel Winning asked me to do this; it was standard procedure to brief new commanders.

The Bensheim camp bothered me. In June, I had permitted the temporary transfer of two Jewish doctors from our Langenzelle camp to Bensheim, where there was a shortage of medical personnel. The stipulations were clear: they were to be regarded as UNRRA staff, with separate housing, pay, living quarters, meals, and sanitary facilities. The arrangement was neither complex nor unusual.

Unfortunately, it didn't work. After about three weeks, the Jewish doctors approached me, asking that they be allowed to return to Mannheim. The Polish officers shunned them; the priests treated them with contempt; and the girls assigned to do their housekeeping—making beds, washing clothes, cleaning rooms—refused to work for Jews. I phoned the UNRRA director to verify their reports, which he did, and I then advised him that the two doctors would not be returning to Bensheim and that there would be no replacements. That ended that experiment.

But I was still bothered. Anti-Semitism had flourished even when a competent, unprejudiced commander had been in charge. What would happen now? How did this major intend to deal with the legacy of hatred? How did he feel about Jewish DPs? About DPs in general? How did all the new captains, majors, lieutenant-colonels—GIs generally—who were pouring into occupied Germany feel about their jobs, their missions? Did any of them even have a sense of mission?

One of the first things I noticed when I sat down in the major's office was his secretary, an attractive German woman who had accompanied him (I found out later) from his previous post. She stepped into the office, tossed him a coquettish glance, looked up something in a file cabinet, and walked out. I was stunned by her beauty.

Her presence did not surprise me, however. American soldiers found German Fraüleins almost irresistible. They were submissive, obedient, punctual, always correct when addressing an officer, and never hesitant to ease their conquerors' daily tasks with compliments, flattery, often with sexual favors. Moreover, they were neat and orderly. They kept their homes fastidiously clean, lavished affection on their children and pets, respected authority, and obeyed our orders. In short, they seemed to be totally decent people. As the occupation continued through the summer and fall, German women—in fact, most of the German population—were looked upon as embodying many pre-Hitler American views of what Germans were like. And these views were often positive.

German women weren't the only ones to mesmerize the occupying troops. At the Kaiser Wilhelm camp, the Latvian section contained scores of young women whose raw, sensual beauty—tussled blond hair, earthy, erotic manners, provocative looks, and no inhibitions—attracted sex-starved American soldiers like magnets. The Latvians, like many DPs as well as many Germans, were accustomed to bartering sexual favors in return for food, shelter, or clothing; it was a basic law of survival. In fact, I had to dismiss the elected chairman of that group because he had instructed several women under his jurisdiction to sell themselves to American GIs. The assumption was that the appreciative soldiers would respond with gifts, personal attention, or anything that would make life easier for the residents. And the assumption was correct, which is exactly why I had to put a stop to their activities.

"I find it difficult to understand this policy, Lieutenant," the major asked after listening to my brief, opening comments. A mild sneer passed across his lips. "Why all this special concern for the DPs, especially for the Jewish DPs? I mean, they've gone through a lot, but then so has the German population." He leaned back in his chair, eyeing me carefully. "And the Germans are a hell of a lot easier to deal with."

"Sir, it has been our policy, which is SHAEF policy, to treat the DPs with the utmost consideration," I repeated, a bit stiffly. "They are to be treated better than the Germans. Not worse, better. Plenty of food, twenty-five hundred calories a day, the clothing they need, medical treatment ..."

"We give them everything they need, and they don't appreciate a damn thing," he interrupted.

"They've gone through a lot, sir. Much more than you or I can imagine."

"And they're paying back too," he retorted. "Every chance they get, they loot, rape, fight each other and the Germans. And DPs steal anything they can get their hands on—bikes, cars, clothes, food—as if it were their right. They don't respect anybody or anything, and they keep demanding more. And you're saying that we've got to treat these people better?"

The major's impression was representative of that of the majority of new American soldiers recently arrived for occupation duties. I understood their attitude, but I still tried to explain a different perspective on the matter.

"Sir, my section has been dealing with these problems since before V-E Day. Please try to understand that the DPs feel that they're just getting back from the Germans what the Germans took from them. The Germans put them all through hell." My voice raised. "Naturally they're bitter. Wouldn't you be?"

The major looked at me icily. "Of course, I would be; we all would be. But they're still damn difficult to deal with. They're dirty, filthy, troublesome. I can see why the Germans ..."

I waited for him to finish his sentence. He didn't.

"You can see why the Germans what, sir?"

"Nothing," he said.

He didn't have to conclude his thought. The message passed from his lips unspoken: he could see why the Germans had treated the DPs as they had.

I brought his words to their conclusion. "The Germans made the DPs the way they are, Major. They were decent, clean, law-abiding folk before the Germans took everything they had and treated them worse than animals and then slaughtered them." I wanted my comments to sting.

Ignoring me, he said, "Yes, but look at their involvement in black market operations. These DPs are cunning people. Cunning and grasping. The Jews especially."

There was no question that black marketing was rampant among DPs, but it was even worse among the occupation troops. I was not aware of anyone who was not somehow involved in the black market. Countless American soldiers "kitted" their money in France. This practice involved selling dollars to black market operators in Paris for four times their value in francs, then taking their francs to an Army Post Office (APO) and reconverting this currency into American money orders to send back to the States. In fact, I learned that the finance officer in Paris discovered that more money was being sent home by American GIs than was being distributed for the entire payroll for troops stationed in that city! All the APOs in Paris had to be shut down for a month in order to clean up this activity.

Worse, many officers were very good looters themselves. They were more sophisticated than the DPs because they could take advantage of their positions and had more contacts. For instance, when I was in Antwerp I spent a week at the chateau of my former Belgian repatriation officer, with whom I had worked in the early days after the German surrender. It was obvious he had done very well for himself. Upon touring his impressive estate, I saw three expensive German cars that he had confiscated while leading repatriation convoys to Belgium, France and Luxembourg. I also heard of someone who actually inveigled his way into owning a cutlery manufacturing plant in Germany—getting the building, machines, employees, the whole thing! Everyone ended up with something—cars, motorbikes, Lugar pistols (seventy to a hundred dollars on the black market), endless varieties of war souvenirs, not to mention the numerous German Fraüleins. I sometimes felt that every GI in the occupation forces was snaring what he could. Taking advantage of one's stay in Germany to garner as much memorabilia as possible was thus a universal practice.

I must confess to resorting to black market operations myself on occasion, although on a small scale. Occasionally I purchased cartons of cigarettes from an Army Post Exchange (PX) and, since I did not smoke, gave them to a Jewish family living in Paris. They sold them on the black market, and we split the proceeds fifty-fifty. It helped them survive those desperate days, and it helped me enjoy Paris, since I used my share to defray travel expenses. I was not pure, and neither was my staff. But his remarks about Jews were unconscionable. Too often had I heard them being blamed for what everyone else was doing, usually on a much larger scale. Jews were easy marks, easy to use as scapegoats.

"Sir, is it cunning for a Jewish survivor of a death camp to get milk through the black market for his child who is starving? Is it cunning and grasping for a Jewish mother or father to use the black market to get a vegetable, or an apple, or an orange? Many of them have never seen any fruit. Did you know that, Major? A lot of kids I've taken care of didn't know what an orange looked like. Did you know that?"

He stared at me without expression.

I kept talking. "We can't condemn all the DPs, all the Jews, just because they want to enjoy some petty luxury that you and I take for granted— like a chocolate bar, a bottle of wine, or a cigarette. Should they be blamed for doing what most GIs have done since setting foot on European soil? It doesn't seem to me to be cunning and grasping ..."

"Lieutenant, I'm curious," he interrupted. "I've been kind of wondering. Who are you anyway? What are you? What's your background?"

The intent of his question was clear. I had gone through this ritual in civilian life often enough to recognize what he wanted to know. I tried to put him off by explaining a few additional things about his "dirty and troublesome DPs."

"I've seen enough things in my background as an AMG officer to know that your camp at Bensheim is hugely overloaded, sir. You've got three thousand people crammed into a place meant for one thousand. There are seven showers for all of them, all three thousand. And I've been through countless houses in this area. Any German family of four has two bathrooms, three or four bedrooms ..."

He brushed aside my comments with a wave of his hand. "Yes, yes, I know that, but what are you? What is your background?"

"I'm an American, born in New York."

"No, no, that's not what I mean."

"I graduated from the University of Illinois with a Bachelor's degree and law degree. I have a degree from the University of Chicago, School of Social Work."

He gave me a thin smile. "Congratulations, but that's not what I mean and you know it."

Temper rising, I continued giving him information that I knew meant nothing to him. "I've got a wife and two daughters ..."

"That's nice." He started to fuss with some papers on his desk, displaying his obvious disinterest in my answers. We both knew I was playing a game. I decided to end it.

"Do you want to know if I'm Jewish?" I asked.

"Yes," he replied, with a patronizing sigh. "That would explain of lot of things."

"You're damn right I'm Jewish, Major. I'm proud of it. And being Jewish doesn't 'explain' a damn thing. It's SHAEF policy to take care of these people because they're human beings. This has been my job since I've been here, and I'm simply trying to do it." I made no effort to control my temper. "And you have no damn right to ask me a question like that!"

He gave me a condescending smile.

"That's what I thought," he said, letting a mild smirk garnish his answer. "And yes, it does explain things; everything, in fact. This, this ... overblown 'concern' of yours for the camp residents," he emphasized 'resident', giving the word a derisive twist, "comes from the fact that you're Jewish. And you talk about treating the Jews better because you're Jewish." He leaned back, self-satisfied. "Yep. That explains everything."

I stood up slowly, letting my chair scrape the floor with a grating sound.

"The policies I explained to you, *major,* are SHAEF, I repeat, SHAEF policies. Furthermore, they are being carried out by Colonel Winning, who, you will note, is not Jewish. The treatment of DPs in our section is 'explained' simply by the fact that we are following orders. And if you'd been here longer, dealing with DPs on a regular basis, I think you would see that these orders make sense." Turning toward the door, I said, "And the Colonel assumes that the orders will be followed." Then I left.

I reported my conversation with this major to Colonel Winning, adding the recommendation that the new officer be transferred to a more appropriate post. The meeting still troubled me though; it lingered in my thoughts, nagging, haunting, adding to the sense of anxiety I felt for the longer-term DPs in our camps. It especially bothered me that the major was not unique; his attitude was shared by huge numbers of occupation troops that my staff and I had encountered over the summer. Experienced AMG personnel, sensitive to the needs and sufferings of the DPs, would not be in Germany forever. Eventually they would all go home. What would happen then?

About a week after my encounter with the major, he was transferred to the Public Safety section, and I had to go through the same routine with his replacement. There were other replacements too, dozens of them; and they all outranked me. But it was still my job to talk to them. I handled my briefing job by explaining that I was on a mission for my commanding officer to convey his orders about governing the DP camps, and that these orders simply implemented SHAEF policy. Many replacement commanders looked at me askance, not quite believing that the words of a Jewish first lieutenant about the treatment of Jewish DPs represented official policy. One of them even dared to question the colonel about me and received a severe tongue-lashing in my presence for his trouble.

This small victory, although gratifying, was ephemeral and did nothing to relieve my worries. I wondered, my staff wondered, and we all fretted: What would happen to displaced persons, to the survivors of the Holocaust, as the victorious Allied forces changed the guardians of occupied Europe? Also, and I admit that this was a personal concern: What would happen to my big Jewish family if they ever got into the hands of the likes of that major?

The Harrison Report

I had told the major that the only reason we dealt with DPs and Jews the way we did was because of orders, SHAEF policy, which applied to all the Allied forces. That was not entirely true. In fact, the way DPs were handled depended heavily upon the commanding officers of the region wherein their camps were located. Some of these places were notorious, such as those under General Patton's command.

But he was not the only high ranking officer to exhibit disdain for the problems of DPs and Holocaust survivors; there were many others. On July 22, the World Jewish

Congress, after reviewing the DP situation in Germany and Austria, announced that "the condition of Jews under Allied control is the same as before except that they are no longer subject to torture and murder." Barbed wire enclosures, armed guards at the gates, passes to come and go, crowding, inadequate food, and skimpy, often filthy sanitary facilities characterized the living conditions of many camps under American occupation.

The attempts of the World Jewish Congress to publicize the deplorable conditions of many DP camps were supported by similar efforts by other groups and individuals. Sympathetic military personnel sent letters home expressing shock over what they had seen; important observers representing large organizations in the United States conducted tours of the American occupation zone; reports from all sections of Germany under American Military Government—Vienna, Berlin, Frankfurt, Salzburg, Munich, Bavaria—filtered home and surfaced in American newspapers and magazines. Shocked by such accounts, President Truman responded by appointing Dr. Earl Harrison, dean of the University of Pennsylvania Law School, to head a task force in charge of investigating the DP problem. He began his mission in late June and completed it in early August.

I was privileged to conduct him on a tour of some of our camps, Kaiser Wilhelm Kaserne in Neckarstadt and the home of "my Jews" at *Schloss Langenzelle*. He inspected the facilities, ate in the dining halls, met with the governing councils and chairmen, and conversed with DPs individually and in groups. He also spent a long time chatting with me, discussing the philosophy behind our mission in Germany, and soliciting our views about the treatment of displaced persons and Jewish death camp survivors.

"Camp organization … ," Harrison mulled over some papers, flipping them over and back. "I can see the ones in your jurisdiction are run democratically—within limits, it seems."

"Yes sir," I answered. I had conducted tours of our camps before, but some visiting dignitaries insisted on going on their own—no intermediaries, no resident 'official' explainers, nothing to muddle the clarity of their first-hand observations. Harrison was one of these.

Another such was General Walter Bedell Smith, who had visited Kaiser Wilhelm Kaserne back in June. After briefing him about our operations, I had offered to take him on a tour. Without responding, he turned to the major who had accompanied him, a public health nurse, and gruffly told her to inspect the facilities. "You know what to look for," he advised. Then he followed her to carry out his own investigation. Lieutenant Plessner and I waited for them in my office, a nervous self-confidence pervading our thoughts. They both returned expressing satisfaction with what they had seen, but the general had one reservation.

"How come you're buying fresh eggs and milk from the Germans? There's a directive against that, Lieutenant."

"We only use that for the children and sick in the hospital, sir."

"So what? I've got ulcers, and I still eat powdered eggs and milk. Why can't they, too?"

"I was informed by our medical officer that the real stuff is healthier for children and for those in the hospital. So I thought …"

"Cut it out and stick to the directive," he ordered, getting up and walking toward the door. Then, turning to me as he left, "You still got a damn fine place here, Lieutenant."

"Thank you, sir."

A few days later, a sergeant from SHAEF came by to inform me that, after checking with his own medical personnel, the general was now authorizing our use of real milk and eggs for the young and infirm. I appreciated that. And I respected him. He was tough and direct, but fair.

So was Harrison, President Truman's special investigator for the DP situation. "The camp commander is quite a character," he offered. "I'm glad to see you all get along. Believe me, that's refreshing after what I've seen in the rest of the country."

He was referring to Kal Plessner, of course, who was indeed a marvel to watch at the camp meetings. Plessner was not only the oldest second lieutenant in the army (I thought), but also one of the smartest and most theatrical. Master of a half dozen tongues, he chaired the weekly council meetings with the flair and body motion of a conductor directing a symphony. With crisp, snappy gestures of his swagger stick, he called for reports from one nationality after another, listened to their comments, succinctly translated the results, answered questions, and then moved swiftly to a different group. Part commander, part conductor, and part entertainer with a thick slice of ham, Plessner dazzled them all.

"Once in a while he thinks he's under orders to provide some comic relief," I answered, unable to think of anything intelligent to say.

Harrison laughed. "How do your meetings work out generally, Lieutenant? Any problems?"

"Generally no, or at least nothing we can't handle. The camp meetings almost always go well. If there are problems to solve, we solve them; or rather, they do, the residents. Sometimes we have to come down hard, if rules are broken or somebody gets out of line. Other times, we use a lighter touch."

"What do you mean?"

As I offered these remarks, I wondered how much I should try to explain. No matter; a person as sharp as he would find out anyway.

"One time early in the occupation, before V-E Day, we had some problems with missing supplies from our warehouse in Neckarstadt."

Harrison showed no expression. Clearly, he had heard of such things before. "Serious?" he asked.

"Sometimes."

"Were DPs involved?" He was aware of all the accusations against "thieving DPs" or "cunning and grasping Jews." I wanted to clarify the matter quickly.

"On occasion, sir, but not extensively. More than not, we had to stop the looting carried out by repatriation officials—the French, for instance. They managed to siphon off several shipments of shoes before we caught them. But DPs have been involved too."

"In what way?"

"It depends on the group. One time we teamed up with the Russians to raid their camp in Heidelberg and ended up netting trucks full of black market goods, and a lot of AMG vouchers, too." I briefly explained the incident at Heidelberg, not wanting him to generalize too much from it. "That was more serious, of course," I continued, "but we've had things happen that are kind of funny, too, when you think back."

"I haven't heard too many of those yet," he said. "Tell me."

I was glad to get to this story. "A group of Jewish concentration camp survivors from Greece ended up in the camp you just visited ..."

"Kaiser Wilhelm ..."

"Yes. After they recovered, I put them to work in the warehouse. It gave them something to do, and Sergeant Roe—he's in charge over there—needed some light help. He ended up with more than that. Now picture this ...."

I smiled, and Harrison returned it, anticipating, enjoying the change in mood. "Roe called me up and asked me to watch these guys leave the building. It was hotter than hell, and these Greek Jews were dressed to the gills with heavy overcoats. They all looked like fat, overstuffed penguins. They could hardly walk. We stopped them. Roe ordered them to unbutton their coats. They did it, giving us funny looks, you know, embarrassed. Hot, fat, sweating—they were a real sight. They opened their coats and sprinkled the ground with cans, dozens of them. They'd taken them from the broken cases and apparently were going to open them up at the camp. It didn't look like a black market thing to me—it was too obvious."

"So what did you do?"

"Well, pilfering goods from an AMG warehouse must be regarded as a serious matter, and I treated it that way, even though I wasn't really that mad at them. So I gave them a little lecture, told them that they could be punished for theft, and then made a deal with them. I knew they weren't going to be there too much longer anyway."

"What sort of deal?"

"We kept empty barrels to store odd lot goods that fell out of broken cartons. I told them that at the end of each day they could take as many cans as they could lift out with their hands. And that worked; they didn't steal any more." I chuckled. "But there was an increase in the number of broken cartons, and that kept the barrels full."

Harrison smiled. "No surprise."

"Yeah, there are worse things, much worse—a lot of resentment against DPs by our own troops as well as the Germans, shoddy treatment of them … , a lot of anti-Semitism, too. Some of it is pretty vicious."

"So I've seen," he agreed. "I've been meaning to ask you—what has been your experience with UNRRA? I see there's an UNRRA staff at Kaiser Wilhelm. They seem quite efficient, friendly."

"They are, but I've been fortunate." I returned. Then I rattled off the names of UNRRA personnel who had done excellent jobs in my district. Ethel Ostry at Kaiser Wilhelm Kaserne; Alex Squadrilli, UNRRA deputy director for the Seventh Army; David Wardlinger, his assistant; Eric and Betty Tobias, a married couple who worked at Langenzelle and were former DPs saved by a "righteous Christian" family during the war. "All of them are sensitive and caring people as well as competent. But they're also exceptions. Many of the UNRRA people are … questionable." I let my sentence trail off.

"That bad?"

"Much of the time, yes."

UNRRA, the acronym for the United Nations Relief and Rehabilitation Administration, was organized in 1943 to carry out the activities its name implied—relief for war-torn Europe and rehabilitation of its victims. Its primary purpose was to complement the AMG mission to care for DPs and eventually to displace army personnel completely and administer the DP camps alone. It was also an umbrella organization designed to coordinate the efforts of numerous private relief agencies—the Red Cross, American Joint Distribution Committee, Catholic Welfare, American Friends Service Committee, and others. UNRRA personnel were organized in teams representing forty-six countries. They were in all the camps, working with military personnel, and I had dealings with them regularly.

"Mostly lack of preparation," I said, in answer to his next question, "insufficient background and training. They don't know the country very well, can't speak the languages, and don't have the necessary skills to deal with DPs' needs. A lot of them have carried their own prejudices to their work and hate the DPs and Jews almost as much as the Nazis. I even heard one say that Hitler should have killed every one of the Jews and saved us all this trouble. Incredible! Can you believe that?"

Harrison just stared at me. I really didn't expect an answer to this impromptu outburst; none was forthcoming.

I continued, trying to put on a more professional demeanor. "Most UNRRA staffers don't have any concept of mission. If there's one thing that has driven us, motivated us, it's been a sense of mission. More than that, a crusade. I don't think anyone who has worked with the homeless and with concentration camp victims on a regular basis can help but become totally immersed in their needs, and with the desire to help, to bring their worlds together again as much as possible." I shrugged. "Call it a quest for justice if you will. That's how we feel. We are dealing with those who have been victims of the most colossal injustice in history. But most of the UNRRA people don't really look at their presence here in that way. They just view this as another job, an easy one with few expectations. It gives them a chance to have some excitement in a foreign country; it gives them some power over people. That especially bothers me. I've talked about this a lot with the really excellent UNRRA folks, the ones I just mentioned ..."

He nodded.

"... and they seem to think that, in fairness to the organization, it had to recruit from forty-six countries as fast as possible. It had to grow too quickly to find the right people. UNRRA leaders ended up taking almost anyone they could find, and they still ended up short." I paused. "Probably their best are as good as our best, Dr. Harrison. But their worst are horrible. I also think ..."

"I understand what you're saying, Lieutenant," Harrison interrupted. He gave me an understanding look that I appreciated. Perhaps he wanted to relieve my obvious distress at having to review actions that I considered an affront to my profession, to the dedication shown by my staff and colleagues in charge of repatriation. "General Michelson at SHAEF has gotten rid of a lot of UNRRA personnel, for exactly the reasons you cited," he offered.

Although I was aware of that, Michelson's action provided small comfort to me at that time given the number of officials involved and the "horror stories" about their conduct that regularly filtered into my office. However, I later learned that by the end of the year the general managed to dismiss almost one thousand UNRRA staff members for incompetence, inefficiency, and misconduct.

"Let me just suggest," I concluded, "that the average level of competence among UNRRA staff is still below AMG personnel, and sometimes our troops don't know terribly well what they're supposed to be doing, especially the replacements we've been getting over the summer."

Bad ending, I thought. The last comment had slipped out before I had had time to think about it.

"So I've seen," Harrison responded simply. Our discussion continued until it was time for his next appointment. He got up, we shook hands, and he left.

I found Dr. Harrison's questions probing, and his temperament, compassionate and just. He impressed me enormously as a person determined to ferret out the truth and to speak honestly about it, regardless of the consequences. I wondered how much of what he had learned would be embodied in his final report.

It was all there. Dr. Harrison's conclusions about the status of DPs in the occupation zones were devastating. After touring camps in Germany and Austria, he issued a report excoriating the practices that left most DPs in situations not much different from those in which they had suffered when the Nazis were in power. Singling out Jews for special consideration, the report stated acidly that "one is led to wonder whether the German people, seeing this, are not supposing that we are following, or at least condoning Nazi policy." He dwelt on the lack of rehabilitation programs: "Camp inmates have little to do except to think of their plight, the uncertainty of their future and what is even more unfortunate, draw comparison between their treatment under the Germans and now in liberation."

Harrison was further dismayed to find that most AMG officers seemed more concerned about getting Germany running again and less interested in dealing with the victims of Nazi atrocities. Too many commanders did not want to inconvenience the German population, he felt. By implication, AMG authorities had much the same perspective toward Germany's displaced subject peoples as the Nazis—new masters, old views. In short, the Harrison Report was a scathing indictment, embarrassing, humbling. President Truman, by all accounts, was genuinely shaken by it. The chief executive's path, should he decide to take it, was clear.

He did. President Truman issued directives to SHAEF to act upon the Harrison Report immediately. General Eisenhower ordered the necessary changes in line with Harrison's recommendations, and by August DP camps in the American zone of occupation underwent sweeping changes. DPs were no longer to be treated as criminals or prisoners of war—no more barbed wire, armed guards, ragged, filthy clothing, and substandard meals. Eisenhower insisted that the conditions for DPs were to be improved by commandeering German homes, hotels, apartments—whole villages, if necessary. Commanders who showed, as the Harrison Report put it, "utmost reluctance or indisposition, if not timidity, about inconveniencing the German population" were replaced by others who followed orders. Acting upon Harrison's recommendation that Jewish survivors "should have first claim upon the conscience" of the American people and military authorities in Germany, he ordered that separate facilities be provided for them.

The Harrison Report was complimentary to our section in that it justified the practices we had been carrying out since the early days of the occupation. We did not feel particularly noble, however, and none of us drew any satisfaction from having our worst fears confirmed about the situation in most of the other DP camps. I had always been confident that our unit in Mannheim had a good grasp of the situation, better than that of many in positions of authority who had not really investigated the horrors experienced by the victims of the Nazis or thought seriously about what was required to help them. And I had been particularly fortunate to have been able to serve under commanders—Colonel Winning as well as his successor, Colonel Lisle—who were astute as well as compassionate and who had given me the freedom to act according to what I thought was right and just.

Sometimes, though, being convinced that your approach is just doesn't give you the means to act that way. The forced repatriation of the Ukrainians, for instance, was egregiously unjust; but we were helpless to stop it. Accounts of displaced persons treated like common criminals, imprisoned behind high walls and barbed wire, prodded by weapons to march like sheep to the slaughter, herded on railway cars like cattle—these things made all of us feel sick and helpless. As the summer wore on, I wasn't even sure I could continue to look after "my Jews."

Where could they go?

Chapter Six

Departures

The Last Move

"Stuttgart will be fine."

"Are you sure?" I asked.

"You mean, aside from having no choice?" Ethel Ostry replied.

She didn't have to remind me of that. Our section had been directed by headquarters to relocate the inhabitants of *Schloss Langenzelle* to Stuttgart, a move I felt was dubious. It sent me scurrying to the map to see if I could spot anything that looked big enough—government buildings, apartment complexes, a few blocks of residential housing, anything—

to accommodate all the Radomers. Stuttgart had been hit hard by our bombers, and there was no assurance that whatever I could find on the map would still be standing. My previous visits to the city did not leave me optimistic, but I trusted Ethel Ostry's judgment.

"What's the bomb damage like? Anything left standing worth moving into?"

"Really, Al, it's not too bad. I walked around the whole complex, every building, and there are just a few areas that aren't usable."

She gave me a bright, enthusiastic look and a detailed review that brushed aside my doubts. The main structure of the apartment complex she had investigated was divided into self-contained flats, which permitted the sort of family life environment the Jewish DPs had missed for so many years. Other buildings in the area could be used for classrooms, workrooms, a library, perhaps even a synagogue. I complimented her work and busied myself to prepare the Radom Jews for the move. They all loved the castle, but the more far-sighted among them wondered anxiously what would happen when their temporary home was returned to the countess. This was precisely the problem I thought we had solved.

As I left my office, I bumped into Chaplain Hasselkorn.

"I think we got it, Abe. We have a place."

"So I heard. I chatted with Ethel on her way out."

"I can't wait to tell them. I'm on the way to the castle now. Can you go with me?"

"Sorry, too many 'clients'," he smiled, nodding in the direction of his office. Then, more serious, "What else are you going to tell them?"

"What do you mean?"

"They're not the only ones who are leaving."

"Oh, yeah. Well ... , one thing at a time."

"That's what you don't have—time."

He was making me feel uncomfortable. "I haven't sorted things out yet." I paused, and we stood there briefly, looking at each other.

"Let me know how it goes," he said, turning toward his office. "I'll see you when you get back."

I waved him off, hopped into my jeep, and rumbled down the streets of Mannheim, off to see "my Jews" at *Schloss Langenzelle*. I was troubled and excited at the same time.

Stuttgart has to work, I told myself—maybe for a long time. The "old guard" AMG people were leaving, myself included.

My meeting with the camp residents did have its complications, however. Most of the Radomers were relieved that we had found a new residence, but a strong minority protested any move whatsoever. Some felt that the plight of Jewish survivors would make a more dramatic impact upon world opinion if they stayed at the castle; others were simply fearful of any change and preferred their present situation to another leap into the unknown. I sympathized with them, but still had to advise them that we had no choice. A delegation was appointed to survey the new area, and their cheery report relieved the anxieties of those who wanted to remain. The date for the move was set for late August.

There was one last request made by the camp council on behalf of the residents. They wanted a memorial service at *Schloss Langenzelle* to honor the memories of their loved ones who had not survived the Holocaust. We readily agreed, and the service was held the evening before the move.

American soldiers and UNRRA officials attended, their respectful visages dotting the congregation of camp residents, all immersed in thoughts and prayers. The cavernous room glowed softly, bathed in the pale light of candles placed on a white cloth over a large table near the front. The candles represented the departed souls of the Holocaust, lit in their memories. The steady, elegant light suffused the room, hushing movements, soothing thoughts, gracing even the shadows with quiet dignity.

I entered the sanctuary with Ethel Ostry and Lieutenant Plessner. Marek Guttman, who presided over the service, asked me to take a place beside him. His eyes, dark and intense, reflected the candle's glow. When all were assembled, Guttman rose to address the participants in the service. All eyes focused upon him. As he spoke, his voice penetrated the room. My thoughts anchored onto his words, moving with their rhythm.

> Ladies and gentlemen! In the name of all former prisoners of our camp, I have the honor to welcome our dear guests, especially our commandants, Lieutenant Hutler and Lieutenant Plessner, and the ladies and gentlemen from UNRRA.
>
> Our meeting today is arranged by the occasion of the third anniversary of the deportations from Radom, for the memory of its victims, our relatives, our loved ones, who were shot on the streets or sent to Treblinka to be killed and burned. It seems tiresome to repeat

these terrible stories, but we know it is our obligation to fight always and everywhere against this unspeakable barbarism, not only for us, but also for our friends who have liberated us, and for all the peaceful nations of the world.

Three years ago, Radom, the native town of most of our comrades, was evacuated by SS troops. We had suffered before, but this three years began what seemed like an eternity of anguish. We remember and see still the bloodthirsty, black demons, the Nazi bands, who tore our families out of our beds at night and drove us into the streets, which became a battleground.

I recall, as you all do, twelve o'clock midnight, one night. I hear neighbors screaming, calling for help. I listen more; I hear shouts, the tread of boots, the sound of marching feet outside, on the streets of our town, Radom. I hear commands cracking like rifle shots, fierce, hate-filled: "Those who have life cards line up here; those without, over there!" People rush to obey. What move means life? What move means death? We see searchlights, cutting our eyes, roving the streets. The lights move, vision returns, slowly. Twisted, vicious faces of our captors fill our views. Executioners they are, waiting to butcher us.

Pistol shots, whips—my heart stands still as I hear them, cracking, killing, slaughtering our people. Youngsters, adults, lying down in their own blood, dead, murdered by the SS. Children thrown against buildings and dropping dead on the streets and the alleys. Everywhere on the streets, a slaughterhouse. People who were not murdered were put on wagons and sent to Treblinka. Over half of them died on the way. Treblinka—the killing place. Our families to the gas chambers, the crematoria. Our women, children,

> screaming, gasping their last breaths ... We see them! We see them!

Guttman swept his arm across his body in a wide arc. The candles flickered in response. He paused for a moment and quietly cleared his throat. There was no sound in the room. The candles recovered and continued their watchful glow, their radiance, intense, attentive.

> We still smell their burned bodies; their ashes are yet in our eyes. I do not wish to detail the cruelties; mere words fail us. We must express our conviction, hard and unshakable, that we shall not, cannot, ever forget.
>
> Radom was a light of Jewish culture, a beacon across Europe and the world. The Nazis blacked out that light. They murdered those who gave light. They wounded those of us who remain. What shall we do? Is it too late?
>
> No, it is not too late. We must not be without hope. We must strive to rise again, we survivors. We owe that to the memory of our dearly beloved dead who had the same yearnings to give light. We owe it to them to spend our remaining days in creating, in building worthy lives again.
>
> Our sufferings will be written into the record of history. They will provide a lesson to all men. Books will be written in memory of the events we have lived through. And thus we will rise up again to be the standard-bearers of high ideals and human brotherhood ....

Guttman finished his message. The sun had gone down. I heard the sounds of men and women weeping without shame. I found myself doing the same. One of the camp residents began to intone the Kaddish, and soon the room was full of the prayer for the dead. Other speakers followed Guttman. Finally, a poet concluded with a stirring cadence of suffering and renewal. The memorial service came to a close, and the congregation departed in silence.

The following day was moving day, from Langenzelle to Stuttgart, a distance of thirty-five miles. Trucks were filled with camp residents, with their belongings and supplies. A horse and wagon took its place near the rear of the convoy, its simple, rustic outlines standing out against the line of motor vehicles. I had no idea how the Radomers made this acquisition, and since I hadn't received a complaint, did not inquire. Sergeant Weiss and I left early to get to Stuttgart before the convoy arrived. When it did arrive, the horse and wagon came loaded with fresh produce and fruits, which the Radomers had received in trade for cigarettes, chocolate, and some of their rations.

Their spirit of enterprise made me smile. They'll do fine, I thought. If they just get another chance, they'll all shine as they did before.

In the following weeks, the Stuttgart facility developed into a model of DP camp organization. Each apartment unit was self-contained—kitchen, dining room, two or three bedrooms, and bathroom with flushing toilets. Schoolrooms, library, medical facilities, supply rooms, and recreation rooms for concerts and plays were established, along with shops for various services such as tailoring and shoe repairing, including even a beauty parlor. The camp was run democratically, as it had been at the castle, under the watchful but rarely necessary supervision of UNRRA. Marek Guttman was again elected president, and he and his council immediately set about making arrangements for the eventual emigration to Palestine. This task became more formidable as the camp grew to over two thousand residents. Like Langenzelle, the Stuttgart camp became a magnet for wandering Jews looking for a place to begin their lives anew.

"Many of them are still scared, though," Hasselkorn said to me as I sat behind my desk, scanning one of the council's recent reports. "That's why I don't think I would say anything to them now, particularly after the last visit—you know, General Keyes. General Michelson came the day after that, but a guy like Keyes always sticks in your mind more. It's unsettling."

"I'm going to have to talk to them sooner or later," I replied. "I've been putting it off long enough."

"Have you made up your mind yet?"

I leaned back in my chair and looked out the window. "Yes, I have. I'm going home."

Hasselkorn nodded. "What about the prospect of a promotion?"

"I still want to go home. Plus, you know how I feel about how they've handled that."

"I guess I can't say I blame you." He grinned, "I'm still shocked that AMG is included."

"So am I."

The army had announced that officers could return home sooner than expected, and the surprise was that

American Military Government personnel were covered by the new regulations as well. I had expected to stay in Germany for several years, eventually having my family shipped over so that we could live together during my tour of duty. But the new policy made us all rethink our options.

"Where do you stand on the list on points?" he asked.

"Around the middle, I think."

I pulled out some sheets of paper on which I had done some figuring, stared at them for a moment, and then handed them to the chaplain. The new regulations created a point system based upon the number of years in the service, years of overseas duty, decorations, battle stars, marital status, and number of children. Officers with the highest number of points went home first. I had three and a half years of present duty, eight years of ROTC and reserves, a bronze star, five battle stars, and three dependents.

"You're right," he agreed, "around the middle. And that's with no promotion."

"Four times, Abe," I wagged my finger, "four times requests for my promotion went upstairs. And four times they couldn't find the file. Now I'd like to go home," I sighed, "and *now* they find my file and put my name on the list, near the top. I don't understand it."

"Wasn't it the bottom line that you'd get promoted if you stayed?"

"Yes, up to major, even. But I'm not interested any more. Tell me about Keyes' visit." I was eager to change the subject. "And then Michelson."

The chaplain frowned. "Ethel didn't have too many good things to say about Keyes. His attitudes are a lot like those of the replacements we've been getting."

That's the other reason why, I thought, I want to go home. Working with untrained people who knew nothing about the situation here was discouraging. Still, I felt guilty; I was deserting the people I had pledged to help.

"He said he thought they were lazy, had too many privileges, like cooking in their rooms—you know, stuff like that," the chaplain continued.

"Michelson was better, you said?"

"Ethel said," he corrected. "He was a real gentleman—asked about their rations, chatted with them in their rooms, even helped them get some razor blades from some German barbers so they could set up their own barber shop. He was just a real kind, understanding guy. Really helpful."

"Let's hope for more Michelsons," I said.

Hasselkorn got up to leave. "Pretty soon it'll be out of our hands, Al. Which is why you're going to have to chat with them. Time is getting short."

He was right. In late August, our AMG section was advised that we were no longer directly responsible for *Land Württemberg,* the military district where the Stuttgart camp was located; we had supervisory authority only. Several weeks later, we lost even that, and my official duty to watch over "my Jews" had come to an end. Whether I stayed in Germany or left, it made no difference. All my fretting about how they would react to my departure had come to naught. The Radom Jews and those who had joined them were in the hands of other authorities.

Perhaps it's for the best, I thought. Throughout the hectic and intense months of transporting DPs, I had tried not to become callous to individual needs while attending to the requirements of the many; but when a young Jewish girl, a refugee from Poland, had once pestered me about something she wanted, I lost patience and brusquely dismissed her. She gave me a look that turned my soul, and said that maybe I was too big to think about individual problems—too big, too important, too concerned with the masses. I stood there and stared at her until she finally turned and walked away.

Her accusation deeply unnerved me. I was proud of my section and what we had accomplished. But I wondered, had my experience changed me? Had I become stuffy, arrogant? Mighty Lieutenant Hutler, DP chief extraordinaire, able to ship out masses by the tens of thousands—but only masses, not individuals. Maybe I had changed.

It was time to leave.

I still managed to visit my big Jewish family frequently, however, and each time I learned something that made me more apprehensive. Shortly after my ties were cut from Stuttgart, UNRRA officials completely took over internal administration of the camp from its elected council. But they were not completely in charge. The new AMG officer in charge of the Stuttgart camp issued commands that frustrated everyone living in or connected to the DP camp. The family atmosphere that Ethel Ostry, my staff, and I had struggled to create for the Radomers was ruined by orders requiring all residents to have their meals in a central dining room. Other orders similarly restricted the members of the camp, regulating their freedom of movement and ability to conduct their own affairs. They all wondered what was going to happen next.

Fortunately, a visit by General Eisenhower in late September resulted in a number of dramatic changes. Near the end of his tour of the camp in late September, Eisenhower addressed the residents assembled on the grounds and expressed his satisfaction over what he had seen. I stood behind him, along with Marek Guttman, Colonel Newman, the commanding officer for AMG Württemberg, and the lieutenant colonel in charge of the camp. When Eisenhower finished his speech, he turned to Guttman and said how wonderful it must have been for them to lead normal lives again, to live in their own apartments, prepare food in their own kitchens and eat in their own dining rooms. Marek agreed that it had been wonderful when they were indeed able to do those things, but that everything had changed when the lieutenant colonel took charge.

"It's all centralized now," he lamented, "like a big barracks. Nothing family about it at all. We eat in a central dining room. Our meals are made in a central kitchen." His sad face rolled off frustration and disappointment. "It's as bad as before," he concluded. "I mean, before liberation."

Eisenhower's eyes flashed with anger. Turning to Colonel Newman, he asked, "Is that true?"

The colonel looked at the lieutenant colonel in charge of the camp, who responded with a quick, nervous jerk of his head. Colonel Newman relayed the information to Eisenhower. "Yes, it's true, sir."

Ike's broad, Kansas smile flattened, becoming thin and taut, snapping to attention, it seemed, ready to assert his authority. "If I had an officer that stupid," he stated crisply, "I would dismiss him from that assignment."

And so the officer was. Colonel Newman relieved him of his command on that same day and appointed a new commanding officer, who restored the living conditions to what they had enjoyed before.

However fortunate the effects of Eisenhower's visit, the policy changes had highlighted everyone's main fear: the fate of the Radom Jews depended upon whoever was in charge of them, and nothing else. Whatever might happen after the move to Stuttgart was out of my hands, and after I left, I would see them no more.

Or so I thought.

A Journey Homeward

I received orders to report to Antwerp, Belgium, on October 4 to ship out to the United States. Shortly before I left, a large group of people headed by "my Jews" held a farewell party on my behalf at Kaiser Wilhelm Kaserne. My staff, my interpreters, numerous UNRRA personnel, several of my commanding officers, DPs, and former DPs from all over the American zone were present. The occasion was a marvel to me.

Here they are, I thought. All of them. They're all here in this room. Not masses, individuals. My big Jewish family here to bid me good-bye. How I love them!

I table-hopped around the room, exchanged hugs and kisses with everyone, with all those who had become, in the words of that Radom Jew in Neuenberg, my "big Jewish family," and tried with no success to keep tears out of my eyes. My friends complicated this task by presenting me with numerous letters. Their words moved me deeply; several letters stand out, particularly the one that ended as follows:

> We, the undersigned, are sending you this friendly message in the highest spirits and full of courage because we know that this message is going to a real friend, a comrade who now finds himself in a blessed land far away across the ocean but would still remember the days we spent together and whose Jewish heart will beat for us in this far away land and will deliver our message to our friends, Jews and non-Jews alike, all those who understand us. We send our heartiest greetings and most sincere feelings to you, your family, and your friends. We affix our signatures with most friendly greetings and respect.
>
> In the name of the remaining Jewish political prisoners of Concentration Camp Vaihingen …

There were other accolades, letters of appreciation, and plaques filled with names of those who had been under my jurisdiction at one time or another. Handshakes, embraces, gushing appreciation, and regret at my leaving them behind—all overflowed my thoughts, leaving me weepy, happy and sad at the same time.

"We shall see each other again," I said repeatedly, the passion of affection overcoming my sense of judgment of what was possible.

"Yes! Yes!" came responses from all directions. "In America. In Palestine. Again!"

"Shalom, my brothers and sisters!"

"Peace be with you! Shalom!"

"Shalom!"

Warm faces, radiant smiles, tearful hugs—these were all the "decorations" I needed for my stay in Germany. When the evening came to a close, I was physically and emotionally exhausted.

The evening also left me appreciative, and, for the first time, with a mild sense of satisfaction. They had all made a difference to me in ways I found difficult to express. Because of them, I now relished the details of life with deeper gratitude. The ecstasy of their liberation, the rekindling of their sparkling eyes and wide smiles, the renewal of hope after their timeless, living deaths in the concentration camps had brought life into focus for me. Before I adopted my big Jewish family—before they adopted *me,* actually—I had run my life according to schedule, according to a routine. They had invested me with the verve and passion of a *mission.* The army hadn't given me the mission; my big Jewish family had. The tens of thousands of displaced persons had. The army only put me there and made it official.

My decision to return homeward was slightly complicated by a last minute offer by telephone from the army to return for reassignment to Seventh Army Headquarters. My job would be to administer the repatriation of Polish DPs to their homeland. Two promotions would follow—to captain, and then to major—provided that I sign up for another year. I respectfully declined.

A few days later, I boarded a ship for the ocean trek to the United States. For four days I was seasick; we had hit the tail end of a merciless hurricane on the way. Finally our vessel entered New York harbor in a heavy mist. As we approached the city, the fog lifted, gradually revealing the majestic lines of our country's most famous symbol, greeting me just as it had my grandparents many years ago. The glorious lady of the harbor, the Statue of Liberty, was welcoming us back to the land of the free.

I was home again.

Epilogue

My Jews in America

The Stuttgart Incident

What happened to my big Jewish family? Many went to Palestine; many others ended up in the United States. Some of them I encountered again, in the new state of Israel as well as in America. But before they were able to resume control over their lives, they all endured more agonies of survival in the last place I left them, in Stuttgart, Germany.

After most of my AMG outfit had left Europe, I heard horrible reports about the treatment of nonrepatriable displaced persons. As the Western Allies allowed local governments more authority, Germans increasingly oppressed and often brutalized the helpless residents of DP camps—not only in Stuttgart, but throughout all the occupation zones. The stench of Nazism continued to despoil occupied Germany, and Jews were usually the chief victims. But the incident at Stuttgart in late March 1946 was probably the worst. It sickened me to hear the details.

At 6:15 A.M. on March 29, 1946, about 250 German policemen, their dogs, and several American MPs surrounded the area around the Stuttgart DP complex. They announced on a loudspeaker that with American Military Government authority they were going to enter the buildings to search for black market goods. The residents were ordered to leave their apartments and gather in the courtyard. Most of them did so, but several protested vigorously, defying the long lines of black-uniformed police armed with rifles and gripping leashes held taut by straining, snarling dogs. As I read about the scene, I could visualize the terror on the residents' faces. It gave me chills.

A few of the residents heckled the police; some who moved too slowly were pushed down and handcuffed. Someone fired a shot, and a Jewish volunteer policeman was hit in the foot. Shouts and screams followed; insults and profanity spat out at the offenders. A number of DPs scurried back into their apartments and ran back out with pots, pans, sticks, bottles, and cans to pummel the police. The Germans fended them off, returning epithets, slackening their hold on lunging dogs, and waving their weapons.

In the meantime, several police looted the buildings, carrying out cigarettes, canned goods, shoes, personal belongings, and even clothing. The situation got out of control. Several police fired their weapons, wounding two more DPs.

The American MPs stood by and watched. Then, a camp resident, one of the original Radom survivors whose signature is in my book of remembrances, was shot and killed. The outraged DPs were brought under control only after American MPs moved in with armored cars. Order was eventually restored.

Out of this senseless episode came a new policy promulgated by American military authorities: Germans were no longer authorized to police DP centers, a small victory for such a large price. A frank admission that practically everyone in the country was involved in the black market in some fashion would, of course, have undermined Allied authority. Apparently, honesty refreshes more after time passes, when the guilty no longer feel threatened. Occupation policies in Germany after 1945 were quite beyond me, of course, and I felt helpless to affect them. But I did wonder if things would have turned out differently had I stayed there, if my AMG unit had remained in charge. For years afterward I felt guilty about the Stuttgart incident.

Fortunately, most of the Jewish DPs who made it through the war also triumphed over the agonies of survival during the postwar period. A few even made it to San Diego, which afforded me the privilege of again rendering some help in my capacity as executive director of San Diego's United Jewish Fund. There are dozens of stories to tell; let us look briefly at just four. The first is about Ernest Michel and is written in his words. Michel's account covers the period from the time of my departure from Germany to his retirement in 1989 from the position of executive vice-president for the United Jewish Appeal in New York City. The remaining stories are based upon my interviews with members of the Schauder, Flaster, and Strum families and cover longer periods of time.

Ernest Michel

"Shortly after Lieutenant Hutler left Mannheim in October, I met an American press officer, Captain Picard. He knew that I liked to write, and he gave me a job as a reporter on the first German newspaper that was to be licensed by AMG, the *Rhein-Neckarzeitung*, published in Heidelberg. I worked on the paper with Rudolf Agricola and Dr. Theodore Heuss. The latter was elected in 1947 as the first president of the German Federal Republic. Subsequently, I was asked to join the DANA (the acronym for a German news agency, similar to the UP) staff at Bad Nauheim. In November 1945, I was sent to Nuremberg to cover the first major Nazi war crimes trial. I stayed until the end of the trials in April 1946.

"My articles appeared under my by-line, "Ernest Michel, Special DANA Correspondent, former Auschwitz prisoner number 104995." During that period, I met Abe Laskove of the Jewish Distribution Committee (JDC) Germany and learned of the work of that organization. He advised me on the possibility of emigrating to the United States. Jewish cemeteries were being vandalized and Jews were again having a hard time with German government officials. I was therefore quite ready to apply for immigration to the United States under President Harry Truman's DP Act. I was flattered when DANA offered me a major position on its staff, but I turned it down. My application for entrance to the United States was accepted, and in July 1946, I shipped out on the U.S. Marine Flasher from Bremenshaven—destination: New York City.

"From the ship I sent a telegram to Lieutenant Hutler in Chicago advising him when I would be arriving in New York City. When the ship docked, I heard an announcement paging me and asking that I report to the information desk. There I was told that two ladies were waiting for me. I walked down the gangplank and there they were. One was dressed in a Red Cross uniform. They were looking for a child from Germany. When they discovered that I was a twenty-two-year-old "child," they were speechless for a moment; then they recovered and hugged and kissed me. Mollie Auerbach, Captain Hutler's mother, and Becky Silverman, Mrs. Hutler's cousin, took me in tow as if I belonged to them. I was taken to the Hotel Marseilles with other immigrants.

"But I didn't want to stay in New York, so that evening I called Captain Hutler in Chicago. He was so excited to hear my voice that I knew I had come home. He asked me to come to Chicago as soon as possible. After being processed, I told JDC of the Hutlers and their desire to have me come to their home. JDC purchased a one-way ticket for me, and I was on my way.

Al Hutler met me at the train depot in Chicago and took me home to meet and become part of the family—Leanore, his wife, and his two daughters, Susanne and Frankee Dee. They had heard so much about me that I felt I was already their big brother. It was wonderful to have a family again. We spent the first day getting acquainted, talking about the days in Germany, discussing what I could do, and exploring options for my future.

"I still remember how Al made me an American and initiated me into the American way of life. The second day we toured the city, but before arriving home I was taken to an ice cream parlor. Al ordered a banana split for me, saying that when I finished it, I would have taken my first step toward being an American. I had never eaten anything as delicious as that in my life.

"I wanted to stay in Chicago, and I tried to get a job as a journalist. I went to every newspaper, but there wasn't a job for a new immigrant who was not fluent in English. One day, in desperation, I crashed into the office of Mims Thomason, Midwest chief of the United Press. He became interested in my story, but advised me to look for a job on a small town newspaper. He suggested Port Huron, Michigan; he knew the owner of the paper there. Although I had never heard of that town, I decided to go for it. I spent an eventful year in Port Huron, first as a copy boy, then as a reporter, and finally as a columnist for the paper. The column was entitled "My New Home" and described those things an immigrant found of interest in coming to America. I did a good deal of lecturing in the Saginaw Bay area of the state and made many friends, many of whom I see to this day. On one of my lecture tours, I saw California. The Hutlers had moved to San Diego, California, where Al had become the executive director of the San Diego United Jewish Fund. They suggested several times that I come and stay with them, since they felt that the opportunities were greater in a growing community on the West Coast.

"About that time, I entered a short story contest entitled "My Closest Shave." It was sponsored by the Mollé Shaving Cream Company. Much to my amazement, I won second prize, a new automobile. Since I could now leave Port Huron, I traveled in my new car to San Diego to see the Hutlers. But California brought hard luck along with good luck. I had saved some money from my lecturing fees, and I foolishly invested in a publishing company that was going to make a film, with James Cagney playing the lead. The film never came to pass. I discovered that I had been caught in a scam, and I lost all my savings. It turned out to be a good learning experience.

"I began to go on speaking tours for the United Jewish Appeal, giving me the opportunity to travel all over the United States. My wish to see America had come true. Al then recommended me for a job with the West Coast office of the United Jewish Appeal. The director was Dan Schacht, a very warm and understanding individual from whom I learned a great deal. It was to be a three-month temporary job as a field representative, but it turned out to be the beginning of a lifetime career.

"In August 1950, I married Suzanne Stein, a very attractive young lady who was then eighteen years old. I now have three grown children—Laurie, Joel, and Karen.

"Some ten years after my "temporary" job in Los Angeles, I succeeded my mentor and became the West Coast director of the United Jewish Appeal. From there, I went to New York to the national headquarters of the United Jewish Appeal (UJA), until I was invited, by the JDC, UJA, and the newly created *Appel Unifie Juif de France* (the French counterpart of the American UJA) to go to Paris as their fund-raising consultant. I was in Paris from 1967 to 1970. Two other Americans had been sent to Paris as consultants to the French during the preceding six years but had not been successful. When I left, the French may not have understood or even wanted to accept American methods, but they were raising much more money.

"While I was working in Paris, the Hutlers lived there from 1969 to 1972. Al was JDC's country director for France, and so we were family again and spent much time together until I left in 1970.

"Just before my contract was up, the New York UJA interviewed me for the position of executive vice president, one of the top jobs in American Jewish community life. I accepted the offer, even though my friends told me it was the most difficult Jewish communal position in America, and most probably in the entire Jewish world of communal service. I was told I couldn't last long in that job, but I managed to hold onto it until my retirement in 1989.

"In 1981 I planned, helped organize, and served as chairman of the "World Gathering of Jewish Holocaust Survivors," which was held in Jerusalem. It was a very emotional event , hosting six thousand survivors from all over the world. It received worldwide television, radio, and newspaper coverage. It has also been my privilege to be on television many times and to appear on Abba Eban's program, "Heritage, Civilization, and the Jews." And I testified at the United States Senate hearings concerning the activities of Dr. Josef Mengele. Today I do a great deal of speaking on Jewish subjects, often related to fund-raising, Israel, and the Holocaust.

"I am sixty-six years old as I write these words. America has given me the opportunity to live again, for which I will never cease to be grateful. I hope that I have been able to repay this country to some degree for what it has given me."

The Schauder Family

Three out of five members of the Schauder family survived: Fanny, born in Ulanov, Austria, and her two sons, Jack and Paul. Fanny is approaching ninety years old. Before the war she and her husband, Markus, settled in Worms, Germany, and opened a small department store. The family lived comfortably in Worms and were respected members of the Jewish community. She remembers vividly how on November 10, 1938, the stormtroopers wrecked their store and destroyed whatever couldn't be looted. Their apartment was also ravaged by the Nazis, who even stole their furniture. She said that by then "we had a real fear of what might happen to the Jews, especially since we were trapped in Germany with the borders sealed."

Their apartment demolished, the Schauders joined other Jewish families temporarily living in the Hebrew School adjoining the ruins of what only days earlier had been the famous Rashi Synagogue.

She told me of her experiences during the Holocaust as though she did not want to forget the past. The family continued to live in Worms, shifting from place to place as "the Germans began collecting Jews in 1939, sending them to concentration camps." She continued, "My husband was arrested and held in jail for six weeks and, along with the other Jewish men, was then shipped to Buchenwald. All other Jews, women and children, were told to leave the city. Jack was my oldest at eleven, Hermann, nine, and Paul, eight. Our immediate destination was Frankfurt, where I was separated from my children and sent to Berlin as a slave laborer. I worked in a medical clinic where the doctor was a Jew married to a Christian.

"The boys eventually were moved from Frankfort to a Jewish children's home in Berlin. I felt I was just lucky, but I would have to be alert, maintain my courage, and use my wits if the remainder of the Schauders were to survive." Then she received word from Jack that the Nazis were going to ship all the children to Auschwitz. She passed word to Jack to take his brothers and try to reach the clinic where the doctor's wife said they would be safe.

However, on November 27, 1943 only Paul and Jack arrived at the clinic. When making their escape from the home, Hermann had been taken by the Germans. The next day, when Fanny overheard the doctor's wife calling the Gestapo to tell them the children were there, she and her two boys embarked on an *"untergrund"* existence. They were always illegals, always hiding, always wondering what to do. "I recalled the story of Moses and his mother that my mother used to tell me when I was a child," she told me. "How she put him on the water in the bullrushes. I decided that we would cross the waters to Mannheim, which by that time was *'Judenrin,'* the hateful German description meaning that it was free of Jews. It was that atmosphere, I felt, that would give us a small measure of hope in an otherwise hopeless situation. The Nazis were less likely to suspect any Jews in southern Germany, from which Jews had already been removed."

She began her battle of wits with the Germans and tried desperately to survive with her two sons. The three criss-crossed the country without passes or identification papers, one step ahead of suspicious Nazis—from Berlin to Leipzig to Stuttgart to Mannheim, then to Worms, Karlsruhe, and Ettlingen—always hiding, living in shacks. Some of the time, she recalls, "we even stayed with Nazi bigwigs who offered us temporary shelter assuming us to be homeless Germans due to Allied bombing. Fear and frenzy were our constant companions; it was that state of mind that drove us on day after day. It was a miracle that we managed from one day to the next to escape the ever greater dangers of betrayal and capture. That was the unfortunate end for many thousands of other Jews throughout Germany who had likewise set out to escape the Holocaust."

Finally, the boys hid in Ettlingen, and she, in Heidelberg. When Fanny heard that the American army had entered Mannheim, she knew that the running and hiding were over. She returned to Mannheim, determined to find her boys and begin her life again.

She knew where the boys had been hiding, but there was no guarantee that they were still alive. "Then," she said, "I found you and Chaplain Abraham Hasselkorn who, at my frantic request, drove through the war zone to Ettlingen to search for Paul and Jack. When you found them and brought them back, our reunion was speechlessly ecstatic. We couldn't stop crying with joy." AMG provided the Schauders with a large apartment in Mannheim, well stocked with food, and a normal family life began again.

She assisted other Jews sent to her by AMG, providing them with shelter, food, and clothing. Fanny describes her first Passover in her apartment: "I had forty people for Passover dinner but only one chicken. I made enough chicken soup to serve everyone, which Lieutenant Skitt [a friend of mine] supplied. It was a beautiful evening for Jewish survivors, and it lasted until three o'clock A.M."

I asked her whether she was treated well by the Americans. She replied, "Why not? Why shouldn't I be treated well by the Americans? The Americans were you and Hasselkorn. You two even went with me to Worms and forced the Germans to return some of my belongings and some of the money that I was entitled to. Paul came to your office every day to do odd jobs, take your dog for a walk, keep your desk clean, and earn some money. Of course, I was well treated by the Americans!"

After Hasselkorn and I returned to the States, Fanny was determined to go to America with her sons to begin a new life. I gave her assistance in filling out the requisite forms, and on September 16, 1946, with the help of the Hebrew Immigrant Aid Society (HIAS), the Schauders finally boarded the ship to America. They arrived in New York Harbor, where they were met by their cousins. HIAS provided them with housing at the Marseille Hotel, where they stayed for three months. Their long journey from 1939 to 1946 was finally over.

Paul went immediately to what they thought was our home in Chicago only to find that we had resettled in San Diego. But I managed to meet him in Chicago, and we drove across country to southern California, giving him an opportunity to see the vastness of his new country. After six months, Jack and Fanny joined us, and with the help of HIAS, the family was reunited.

Both Paul and Jack went to public school, Paul into junior high school, and Jack into high school. Fanny secured a job at Ratner Manufacturing, sewing pleats in men's trousers at a piece rate of two cents per pleat, earning about fifteen dollars a week. The boys worked and continued their schooling.

By 1948 Fanny had developed dreams of being independent. "I talked with friends and workers at Ratner's and decided that the way to independence was to own a chicken ranch. As I recall, you spent your weekends driving us around the county looking at chicken ranches until we found one that we could afford in National City. There was an acre of land, about five hundred sickly chickens, some worn-out equipment, and a small barn. The place was generally in such condition that, in your words, no self-respecting chicken would live in it. But it was something we could afford, something that with hard work and determination we could make successful." Fanny financed the purchase with money she had saved since coming to America, a loan from a bank, and a low-interest loan arranged by the Jewish Federation of San Diego from the Jewish Agricultural Society.

Her enterprise succeeded. Fanny explains: "We worked very hard. I continued my job at Ratner's. Paul slept in the shack to protect the property and began work early in the morning before going to high school. Jack and I lived in an apartment. Jack took care of the ranch in the mornings and attended San Diego State University in the afternoon, and I went right to the chicken ranch immediately following my work. It was hard work, but it paid off. Paul developed an egg route. We sold eggs to customers who came to the ranch, and then, as we expanded, we joined the egg cooperative. Within a period of a few years, we had some new equipment, five thousand chickens, and plans for building a home on the property. We bought an additional half acre of land on which to build our home, and, when that was built, we knew America was the golden land."

After the ranch was prospering, Jack entered the air force. He was sent to San Diego State for six months to complete his degree in engineering and never again worked with chickens. Paul continued to work on the ranch while he finished his education at San Diego State and received a degree in accounting and business administration. Fanny finally left Ratner's to work full-time on the ranch. After getting out of the air force, Jack worked for aircraft factories in San Diego for over twenty years. Paul and Fanny continued to develop their chicken ranch until they had about ten thousand chickens. Jack and Paul married, and Fanny is a grandmother of six grandchildren.

Eventually the State of California purchased their land to build a road. They used the money to build shopping centers. Prosperity has been the fruit of many years of struggle.

Today, Fanny lives a very quiet life in her condominium. She helps in the family businesses and uses her strength and determination to keep the family together, just as she did in those horrible days of the war. She says that she still lies awake at night while the past runs through her mind. The little boys who were always on the run and protected by their mother are now grown men living in comfortable homes, with prosperous lives and active families. They are productive citizens and excellent Americans.

Mendel Flaster

Mendel Flaster was born on April 21, 1920, in Grybow, Poland, close to the German border. His wife Geta was born in Bendzin, Poland, in 1927. He lived in Grybow until December 12, 1939, a date that is fixed in his memory as the beginning of his experiences in the Ghetto of Tarnous, Poland. The Ghetto was divided into two sections: "A" where you were sent to die; and "B" where you were sent to work. He was placed in "A," jumped the fence into "B," worked, and managed to survive. He was eventually sent to fourteen camps throughout the war: ten labor camps and four concentration camps—Siebnia, Auschwitz, Buchenwald, and finally Bergen Belsen. He proudly wears his Auschwitz number 161065 on his left arm, saying, "I want to live with it and die with it so that I can show the world what it means." It represents the loss of a father, mother, two sisters, a brother, and two nephews—all murdered.

He spent ten months in Siebnia working with a clean-up team carrying trash to be dumped outside the camp. He established relationships with some Germans and Poles and was able to steal food and bring it back for friends in Ghetto "A." One day he was caught but, for some reason, instead of being killed was given thirty-five lashes and transferred to the death camp of Auschwitz. Flaster said that during his years in the camps he "had been condemned to death twice and both times cried out to God and both times was saved." From there, he was taken to Buchenwald and later to Bergen Belsen. He clearly remembers the April 15, 1945, bombing of the area around Bergen Belsen by both British and American planes. The German guards fled, and British troops entered the camp, liberating the survivors. Tens of thousands had died, and many of those who survived later died from typhus, malnutrition, and other maladies.

Weighing seventy-two pounds, Flaster was taken to a hospital, where he recovered. He then went to Frankfurt in the American zone and was helped by UNRRA and JDC, who found housing for him in a small hotel for Jews. There he became part of the labor group constructing a DP camp in Zeilsheim. When it was completed, he was selected to be part of the camp police. He went to police training in Stuttgart and served with the camp police, AMG Public Safety Section, and the Provost Marshall for several years.

Mendel married Geta in Frankfurt in 1948; their son Abie was born there in 1949. With the help of HIAS, the Flaster family was admitted to the United States, arriving in New York on April 24, 1950. On the following day, they took a journey across America to San Diego, where the Jewish community had promised to welcome them and a brother-in-law had already settled. An additional son was born in San

Diego; a daughter was added later. The local committee found them housing and placed Mendel in his first job in America, as a tailor. From there he went to work in a furniture factory, and leaving that job to open his own tailoring business under the name, California Tailoring. He later sold the business and opened five stores over several years' time. In 1984 he sold the last of his stores and retired.

Manny (as he is called by his friends) and Geta live the comfortable life of a middle-class family. He speaks proudly of the fact that, in the thirty-six years that they have been in the United States, they have never taken charity in any form; only once, in 1952, did he receive an unemployment check. He's repaid his bills and all the loans given to him by HIAS. He is proudest of his family and their grandchildren.

Manny and Geta participate in numerous Jewish community activities, including the local New Life Club of Survivors, the Jewish Community Centers, the Orthodox Synagogue, the Jewish National Fund, and the United Jewish Federation. Geta is an active member of several women's organizations that work on behalf of Israel. Manny has worked for the Hebrew Home for the Aged in San Diego by serving as the leader of their Sabbath services. Since his retirement, he has taken some of the residents out for various trips. He also spends time as a speaker, detailing his experiences for schoolchildren.

He told me that today he is proud of three things: his Auschwitz number, his citizenship, and his economic independence. He expressed his sincere and abiding love for his adopted country: "If I have to give my life to help the United States, I would do so in a minute. America has given me a taste of what it means to be free. I want my children, my grandchildren, and others to be able to taste the same freedom."

He says he still has nightmares, however, even though he knows he is a free man in a free country.

Jack and Frimet Strum

The Strums were born in Zwolen, Poland—Jack in 1913 and Frimet in 1920—both from large families who were in the leather business. In the late thirties, most Jews outside of the Reich were aware of Hitler's designs, and many made attempts to get away. Jack tried to leave Poland but was stopped at the Rumanian border. He returned to Poland only to be drafted into the Polish army, wherein he served three months until the Polish campaign was completed. His town was leveled by the Germans, and most Jews were forced into work details, digging ditches, burying telephone lines, and clearing away the debris. Finally they were sent to slave labor camps to work in ammunition factories.

Frimet and Jack began their lives together under extraordinary duress; they were married in the Jewish Ghetto in Zwolen. They spent their honeymoon in the brick factory where Jack worked. Shortly afterward, the Ghetto was eliminated, and many Jews were sent to Treblinka to be murdered. Jack and Frimet were exceptions; they ended up in the Radom Ghetto. When the Germans closed that Ghetto, they were sent to Shydlowietz, Poland, then back to Radom, after which they were separated. Jack tried to escape but was caught and marched with others over one hundred miles to Tomashow. His journey was continued through other concentration camps, until he ended up at Vaihingen, very sick with typhus. When the French liberated that camp, they resettled the remaining 249 survivors in Neuenberg, where Hasselkorn and I first encountered them. All this time Jack and Frimet did not know whether the other was dead or alive.

Frimet managed to survive Auschwitz, as well as hard labor in an ammunition factory in Lippstadt, Germany. When the Allies approached, she was taken with others on a death march, from which she managed to escape. She was picked up by an American truck and taken to the American zone. She later returned to Poland with an American Jewish chaplain to find her brother, whom she located and brought back to the American zone. She still knew nothing about her husband.

Jack explained their reunion: "I was with the Radomers who were brought from the French zone to Bensheim in the American zone by Lieutenant Hutler. The camp became overcrowded, and we moved to *Schloss Langenzelle* and then to the camp set up by Hutler in Stuttgart. There I learned that my wife had returned to Kolitz. I rushed from Stuttgart to find her, only to discover that she had left Kolitz for Stuttgart to find me! I then dashed back to Stuttgart to find her impatiently waiting for my return. It was wonderful.

"We were both at Stuttgart when General Eisenhower inspected and reviewed the DP camp. I remember that day clearly, the compassion and understanding of the American military leader."

In October 1946, after successfully getting a visa to America, the Strums arrived in the New York harbor, then traveling to Davenport, Iowa. Jack worked in a clothing shop for five years, bought a home, and began raising two daughters. He fell in love with southern California after one visit and resettled there, working with his brother Joe in a business. He retired in 1980. His children are both well educated, with Master's degrees in social services, and live and work in California.

When Jack Strum talks about America, his life in San Diego, and his two girls, his eyes light up. He becomes excited and emotional: "It's the greatest country in the world! No one appreciates it as much as we do. We feel so free here. We've seen very little anti-Semitism and never have been ridiculed for not being able to speak English very well or for having an accent. The police don't stop us for identification papers or ask us where we're going. We've tried to repay America by helping others to the best of our ability."

Jack's eyes got watery when he spoke about his attendance at the Holocaust survivors' meeting in Washington, D.C., in April 1983. President Reagan was the opening speaker. "In what country in the world would the president address a gathering of Jewish survivors? It's simply unbelievable that it can happen. But here in America, it does happen."

He made a point of reading the following words from the president's speech to me. Jack's voice was somber, unbelieving, as he spoke Mr. Reagan's words.

> Tonight we stand together to give thanks to America for providing freedom and liberty, and, for many here

> tonight, a second home and a second life. The opportunity to join with you this evening, as a representative of the people of the United States, will be for me a cherished memory. I am proud to accept your thanks on behalf of our fellow Americans; and also to express our gratitude to you for choosing America, for being the good citizens that you are, and for reminding us of how important it is to remain true to our ideals, as individuals and as a Nation.

"In Remembrance"—A Book of Treasures from My Jews

My most cherished possession is a handmade, hand-printed book from my big Jewish family, presented to me at the farewell party in Stuttgart. The book is entitled, "In Remembrance." It bears the following acknowledgment:

In Remembrance
Our Dearest and Best Friend
First Lieutenant of the U.S. Army
Albert A. Hutler
as an evidence of sincere
Gratitude from the Jewish
political ex-prisoners of
the concentration camp
Vaihingen/Enz Germany

The title page carries a sketch of a survivor in his striped concentration camp uniform, standing behind the barbed wire fence of a concentration camp with barrack buildings in the background. The pages contain photographs of survivors of the Vaihingen camp, signatures of 278 survivors who were living at the Stuttgart DP camp, and a description of a memorial plaque in memory of those who died at the camp.

There are also a number of warm letters, of which one reads as follows:

> Dearest Friend:
>
> After five years of inhuman suffering, a small group of a few hundred men, the total remaining population of 30,000 Jews of Radom, Poland, was liberated by the Allied armies.
>
> Broken in body, soul, and spirit, we found ourselves in enemy country with the days of horror behind us. In our hearts was still a sense of despondency and disaster.
>
> Remembering all our sufferings, we started our new life next to the wires of the concentration camp. The majority of us had not any wives, parents, brothers, sisters, or children left. We remained alone with our disaster, with no one to turn to, longing for a man who would understand us and our sufferings.
>
> Then together with Chaplain Hasselkorn, you came to us. We had the good fortune to meet in you a person who, in a human way, understood us and our disaster.
>
> You didn't come because you were forced to, or because it was your duty, but rather because you were drawn towards us by human feelings and a warm heart. You taught us to walk with our heads high and face the world with pride and courage.
>
> At home we had other friends and still have, but you were the most dear to them all.

You always tried to bring us help in all its forms. Your memory is etched in our hearts forever, and your name will be a living symbol of the proverb, "Love thy neighbor as thyself."

We who have signed our names in this book have done it with a feeling of great happiness and pride because we know that the man who is parting from us is our devoted friend whose heart will yearn for us on the other side of the ocean. To you, dear friend, we say good-bye, and close with the words—we wish you to be blessed forever.

To your family and friends, we send our kindest greetings and friendship.

The book closes with a poem and a letter written by Eugene Gross, a Jewish poet from Czechoslovakia and a survivor of Vaihingen concentration camp. His poem tells the complete story of the Jewish survivor.

Peaceful life, a nice family,
Parents and children, how nice that was ...
Six days work, in our own homes,
The seventh, that was the day of repose.

Then came a man who disturbed this calm,
A beautiful time in Langenzelle had engaged,
Then came suffering, till now unknown,
And the whole world began to flame.

Peaceful men, women, and children,
Stacked in wagons, sick people, old men,
Travel in Transports with hunger and thirst,
Direction—Auschwitz, and unknown fate is awaiting them.

Savage people separate our dearlings,
They take our children and parents away,
They take everything, give only prisoner clothes,
In the background gas and fire prepare for today.

Oh! Black clouds of smoke are arising to heaven,
From the chimney of the crematorium,
Our dearest are all murdered,
Capos are shipping us further through the door.

A long time of pain, we are only shadows,
Hunger and need, beating and cry;
We are not men—as dogs are we treated,
Without our dearests is much better to die.

Thousands of dead each day,
We are alone, see only enemies,
We all are leaded to the sure death,
By weakness, hunger, hard work, and epidemics.

But yet appear flying fortresses,
Escorted by Allied fighter teams,
At the end came glorious armies,
The enemy is in flight and we are free.

Today in the reunion of our dearest guests,
We should like to be joyful again,
From liberated countries return perhaps once more,
Parents, brothers: Our hope will not be vain.

Yet we are not abandoned,
Greatest nations are our Allies.
Sisters and brothers, fathers are our Dear Guests,
Finally to help us is their desire.

Our Dearests! We are so happy,
To welcome you here in our group.
We shall remain always, always grateful,
To you and to our Allies ever true.

APPENDIX ONE

DETACHMENT F1E2
Co E, 2d EDA Regt,
APO 658, U.S. Army

13 April 1945

WEEKLY FUNCTIONAL REPORT
DISPLACED PERSONS

1. D.P. Camps #18 (Mannheim)
   A. Population -(12 April 1945)

1. Nationalities		2. Age	
French	1000	6 mo. to 6 yr.	125
Belgians	645	7 yr. to 17 yr.	118
Polish	666	18 yr & over	5547
Dutch	190		5790

Russians	2663
Serbs	41
Czechs	10
Greeks	280
Italians	295
	5790

During the week the population has shown a fluctuation from a high of 6744 to a low of 4659.

B. Housing

Increased by addition of a block of apartments next to camp. In my opinion camp should hold 6500 people. Camp is in good condition.

C. Food — Condition fair.

D. Health—No health problem; dispensary in good condition.

E. Security—Good — have 40 guards

F. Labor

1. D.P. Camps #18 (Mannheim)— Labor exchange is functioning. Below is a report for the week:

1. Permanent / Temporary

	Permanent	Temporary
Russians	787	413
Poles	252	210
Italians	227	350
Greeks	83	191
Dutch	1	105
French	0	233
Belgians	0	121
	1350	1623

2. D.P. Camp #17 (Heidelberg)

A. Population

French	2500
Belg. & Dutch	600
Russians	2750

B. Housing

Inadequate. The place where the Russians and Poles live is rightly called Hog Hallow. It should be burned.

C. Food — Scarcity soon — at present good. Almost 2000 calories a day.

3. Action Taken During Period

A. Completed agreement for CAS BPA to have labor exchange at D.P. #18 with Major Blount and Major Winkler of CAS. Lt. Purcell of CONAD in charge.

B. Requisitioned block of apartments which can hold 2000 people and put French in them. Conference with Major Cartier, 7th Army OK'd action.

C. On being advised that restriction against moving French had been lifted, secured CONAD transportation through Capt. Wells and Lt. Kline of Transportation Office for moves. French can be transported to:

(a). 1st French Army at Hochenheim — 750 per day.
(b). Repatriation center at St. Avold—1000 per day.
(c). Repatriation center at Saarburg—1000 per day (Hochenheim now closed to us).

Began delousing program at both camps and deloused about 1200 per day through efforts of Lt. Col. Cohen, Major Dodge of 7th Army, and Capt. Hamilton of our detachment.

During this week we sent trucks to both D.P. #18 and D.P. #17 for repatriation of French. Exact figures are not available, because rosters did not completely clear through me.

		From Mannheim	From Heidelberg
To	St. Avold	700	2014
	Hockenheim	2740	729
	Saarbourg		155
		3440	2898

D. Advised by Major Bradbury to take over control of 780 Italians in a former PW camp at Sackenheim. Provided food for them. There is a Pfc in charge and a guard, and a Lt. responsible for them.

E. Sat as court for hearings of D.P. violators of ordinances.

F. Capt. Van Zetten, Holland, and a Russian Lt. reported as liaison officer.

G. Conducted Mr. Dorn of War Department, and Colonel Hezzenbottom through D.P. Camp #18.

Comments:

D.P. Camp #18 is in good shape. In order to take advantage of transportation going to France, will survey possibility of having an assembly point near the Rhine bridge, so that convoys going to France empty can be loaded with personnel in the least possible time.

Thirty-six marriages have been performed in D.P. camp #18 and three births.

ALBERT A. HUTLER
1st Lt., CAC,
Labor & Public Welfare

APPENDIX TWO

Detachment F1E2 AAH/afc
Co E, 2d ECA Regt
APO 658, U.S. Army
21 April 1945

WEEKLY FUNCTIONAL REPORT — Displaced Persons (14 April - 21 April)

General

This was a week primarily of attempting (a) to settle both camps down to a static condition (b) repatriation of French, Belgians, Hollanders, & Luxumbourgers (c) reshuffling of nationalities within the camps (d) movement of DP personnel (e) addition of 3 camps and a hospital (f) to answer questions of DP in relation to Germans (g) entrance of UNRRA into picture.

1. We now have the following organized camps:
   a. Mannheim - Kaiser Wilhelm Kaserne - DP #18 - Capt. Kapp
   b. Heidelberg - Grenadier Kaserne - DP #17 - Capt. Jones
   c. Mossbach - Barracks - DP #112 Lt. Frost
   d. Sinsheim - Dispersed in buildings - DP #108 - Capt. Meyers
   e. Weinheim - In six buildings - I - Lt. Wharton
   f. Heppenheim - Unknown - Capt. Snapp
   g. Heppenheim - 1000 Bed Hospital

2. Population (20 April 45)*

Nation-alities	**Mann-heim**	**Heidel-berg**	**Moss-bach**	**Sins-heim**	**Wein-heim**
Russian	960	5500	1651	1303	948
Polish	1531	150	636	300	633
French	Moving	15**	400**	228**	
	In & Out				
Belgians	30**	150**	61**		
Dutch	10**	200**	64**	31**	
Yugoslav	24			6	25
Czechs	24			4	
Italians	844	19**	154	74	586
Greeks	345	14			12
TOTAL	3768	6048	2966	1946	2204

*Population in Mannheim has fluctuated between 6000 and 3500 but there have been approximately 7000 French, Belg., Hollanders repatriated from Mannheim.

3. Housing, Food, Security, Sanitation, & Medical remains the same at Mannheim & Heidelberg. Mossbach can use a doctor & medical supplies including DDT powder & 2 guns. Will make an effort to secure same. Sinsheim wants DDT powder & 2 guns. Weinheim should have a doctor. Will have UNRRA doctor from Heidelberg report to Weinheim. Believe all camps can handle food problems in our area at present.

4. DP labor at present labor exchange is only functioning in Mannheim Camps.

Permanent		Temporary
Russians	76	454
Poles	24	358
French		33
Czechs		7
Italians	927 ****	504
Greeks	306	12
Total	1333	1368

****This includes 600 Italians formed into (2) labor companies for CONAD units.

AG Major Bradbury is now discussing agreement for use of 1200 Russians from Heidelberg camp.

5. Repatriation Movement (15 April 1945 - 19 April 1945).

From Mannheim			From Heidelberg
To: St. Avold			1175
Saarburg	6089	French	
	444	Belgians	
	413	Dutch	
	6946	Total	

**** Does not include 680 French PW moved direct to Hockenheim.

6. <u>Action Taken During Period.</u>

A. <u>Seckenheim Italian Camp</u> - 910 individuals

Evacuated two barracks and took over three empty buildings near camp. Labor companies released to army units totaling 848 men. Sixty-two men taken to Mannheim camp. Camp completely evacuated, food and beds removed to Mannheim camp. All men completely deloused.

B. Secured commitment from CONAD Transportation for 25 two ton semi-trailers to haul displaced persons from Mannheim to Saarburg (no diversion permitted) from 15 April to 30 April '45. Major Throne of Transportation Group in charge.

C. Moved 1500 French from Bensheim, 750 from Weinheim to Mannheim for repatriation. Cleaned out Bensheim camp.

D. Began shuffling people in order to make Heidelberg all Russian.

E. Received thousands of blankets and comforters at Heidelberg and Mannheim.

F. Cleaned Mannheim area of all French, Dutch, Belgians.

G.Have been moving Poles and Russians to Mannheim camp.

H. Toured area reference DP situation. Contacted:

a. Heidelberg
b. Mossbach
c. Sinsheim

Situation in hand at all places. Many DPs in area are living outside of camp.

7. <u>Future Plans</u>

A. Remove DPs from Heppenheim to Heidelberg and Mannheim.

B. Reopen Bensheim camp (capacity 2000) as an all Polish camp.

C. Mossbach camp to be all Polish.

D. Mannheim camp to be all Russian (Italians are to be fenced off).

E. Wertheim camp (question as to whether or not) to be all Russian.

F. Remove DPs from Weinheim.

G. Remove Poles and Russians from Mannheim area.

H. Two officers and 3 EM from E team are to report to us for assignment as administrators in Heppenheim DP hospital. A French Red Cross Worker (CAS) will be secured from UNRRA to assist.

I. UNRRA doctor in Heidelberg is to be sent to Weinheim to assist the detachment and a French Red Cross Worker (CAS) will be taken there to aid.

J. Mannheim may be used as a clearing area for French, etc. repatriation.

8. Comments

A. We now have Chinese DPs in Mannheim camp.

9. Matters of Policy that Must be Answered

A. Can Germans discharge DPs who have been working for them for some time, in order to hire Germans?

B. Can German authorities refuse billets to a DP when such billet is authorized by a DP (MG) Officer? Does DP Officer have such authority?

ALBERT A. HUTLER
1st Lt., CAC
Labor and Public Welfare

APPENDIX THREE

RESTRICTED

HEADQUARTERS
U.S. FORCES, EUROPEAN THEATRE
LW/LCB/amv
(Main) APO 757

AG 354.1 GEC-AGO 22 August 1945

SUBJECT: Special Camps for Stateless and Non-repatriables

TO: Commanding Generals:
Eastern Military District
Western Military District

1. It is the established policy of this headquarters that stateless and non-repatriable persons shall be granted the same assistance as United Nations displaced persons. This includes ex-enemy nationals persecuted because of their race, religion or activities in favor of the United Nations. Persons discharged from concentration camps, if their loyalty to the Allied cause has been determined, will receive all of the benefits granted United Nations displaced persons even if they were originally of enemy origin, such as German and Hungarian Jews, labor leaders or others put into concentration camps because of political activities or racial or religious persecution.

2. While persons of Jewish faith who desire to be repatriated to the country of which they are nationals will be treated as citizens of that nationality and placed in the same centers as other displaced persons of that nationality, those Jews who are without nationality or those not Soviet citizens who do not desire to return to their country of origin will be treated as stateless and non-repatriable.

3. In accordance with the policy of this headquarters, such persons will be segregated as rapidly as possible into special assembly centers. Those who are Jews will be cared for in special Jewish centers.

4. In establishing these special centers, particular attention will be paid to a high standard of accommodation. Wherever necessary, suitable accommodation will be requisitioned from the German population. Military commanders' powers of

requisitioning will be fully utilized in order to insure that these persons are accorded priority of treatment over the German population.

APPENDIX FOUR

HEADQUARTERS SEVENTH ARMY JLC/ted
APO 758 US Army

AG 383.7-CA 24 August 1945

SUBJECT: Control of displaced persons

TO: See Distribution

1. Reference letter this headquarters, AG O14-CA, subject: Military Government Plan - Germany, dated 26 May 1945.

2. The responsibility of tactical units to maintain law and order includes the authority of local tactical commanders to limit the number of Displaced Persons on pass from centers.

3. Tactical commanders will arrange with the local Military Goverment detachments for the imposition of the necessary restrictions. These shall be the minimum required to maintain law and order.

4. The commanding officers of Displaced Persons Centers will be responsible for the strict complicance with restrictions imposed by the tactical commanders. They will call upon tactical commanders to provide any additional guards required to enforce these restrictions when they are unable to maintain law and order by means at their own disposal.

BY COMMAND OF MAJOR GENERAL WILBURN:

HARRY J.WALTERS
Captain, AGD
Asst Adjutant General

DISTRIBUTION:

"D" plus

MG Det E-1	-100 (1 ea MG Det)
E-2	-100 (1 ea MG Det)
E-3	- 65 (1 ea MG Det)
E2C2	- 15 (1 ea MG Det)
G-5, USFET	- 5
G-5, 7th Army	- 50
AG Records	- 2

APPENDIX FIVE

HEADQUARTERS SEVENTH ARMY
WESTERN MILITARY DISTRICTS
APO 758 US Army

AG 383.7 CA 18 September 1945

SUBJECT: Ukrainian Committees

TO: See Distribution

1. In some areas Ukrainians have been active in organizing committees such as the "Ukrainian Help Committee" and the "Ukrainian Relief Service."

2. Representatives of the Soviet Government have stated that such committees are spreading anti-Soviet propaganda and endeavoring to persuade Soviet Ukrainians not to return to the Soviet Union.

3. The following will be observed by Military Government detachments with respect to these committees:

a. Persons requesting authorization to form groups such as the above will be denied such authorization. Officers or representatives of committees already organized will not be recognized as speaking for all persons in the particular racial or ethnological groups.

b. Ukrainians are not recognized as a nationality and will be dealt with according to their nationality status as Soviet citizens, Polish citizens, Czechoslovak citizens, nationals of other countries of which they may be citizens or as stateless persons.

c. Persons styling themselves as Ukrainians, who are Soviet citizens displaced by reasons of the war, identified by military commanders and Soviet Repatriation Representatives as Soviet citizens, if uncovered after 11 February 1945, will be repatriated to the USSR without regard to their personal wishes, in accordance with paragraph 23c of SHAEF Administrative Memorandum No. 39- Revised 16 April 1945.

d. Persons styling themselves as Ukrainians who are Polish or Czechoslovak citizens will be dealt with under paragraphs 21, 24, 30, or 34 of Administrative Memorandum No. 39 - Revised 16 April 1945, as appropriate.

e. Persons styling themselves as Ukrainians who are stateless will be dealt with in accordance with paragraph 31 of Administrative Memorandum No. 39.

f. Representatives of existing organizations or petitioners wishing to establish committees will be advised that they are subject to Military Government laws and ordinances relating to the prohibition of political activity in Germany and especially to Articles 30, 34, 40, and 41 of Military Government Ordinance No. 1, and that they will be accorded no special privileges with respect to travel authority, transport or communications as compared with other United Nations or neutral nationals in Germany.

BY COMMAND OF LIEUTENANT GENERAL KEYES:

DEAN G. OSTRUM
Captain, AGD
Asst Adjutant General

DISTRIBUTION:

WG Dot E-1	- 150 (1 ea MG Det)
E-2	- 100 (1 ea MG Det)
E-3	- 65 (1 ea MG Det)
E2C2	- 15 (1 ea MG Det)
G-5, 7th Army	- 50

APPENDIX SIX

FROM: President Harry S. Truman

TO: General Dwight D. Eisenhower

DATE: August 31, 1945

My Dear General Eisenhower:

I have received and considered the report of Mr. Earl G. Harrison, our representative on the Intergovernmental Committee on Refugees, upon his mission to inquire into the condition and needs of displaced persons in Germany who may be stateless or non-repatriable, particularly Jews. I am sending you a copy of that report. I have also had a long conference with him on the same subject matter.

While Mr. Harrison makes due allowance for the fact that during the early days of liberation the huge task of mass repatriation required main attention, he reports conditions which now exist and which require prompt remedy. These conditions, I know, are not in conformity with policies promulgated by SHAEF, now Combined Displaced Persons Executive. But they are what actually exists in the field. In other words, the policies are not being carried out by some of your subordinate officers.

For example, military government officers have been authorized and even directed to requisition billeting facilities from the German population for the benefit of displaced persons. Yet, from this report, this has not been done on any wide scale. Apparently it is being taken for granted that all displaced persons, irrespective of their former persecution or the likelihood that their repatriation or resettlement will be delayed, must remain in camps—many of which are overcrowded and heavily guarded. Some of these camps are the very ones where these people were herded together, starved, tortured and made to witness the death of their fellow-inmates and friends and relatives. The announced policy has been to give such persons preference over German civilian population in housing. But the practice seems to be quite another thing.

We must intensify our efforts to get these people out of camps and into decent houses until they can be repatriated or evacuated. These houses should be requisitioned from the German civilian population. That is one way to implement the Potsdam policy that the German people "cannot escape responsibility for what they have brought upon themselves."

I quote this paragraph with particular reference to the Jews among the displaced persons:

"As matters now stand, we appear to be treating the Jews as the Nazis treated them except that we do not exterminate them. They are in concentration camps in large numbers under our military guard instead of S.S. troops. One is led to wonder whether the German people, seeing this, are not supposing that we are following or at least condoning Nazi policy."

You will find in the report other illustrations of what I mean.

I hope you will adopt the suggestion that a more extensive plan of field visitation by appropriate Army Group headquarters be instituted, so that the humane policies which have been enunciated are not permitted to be ignored in the field. Most of the conditions now existing in displaced persons camps would quickly be remedied if through inspection tours they came to your attention or to the attention of your supervisory officers.

I know you will agree with me that we have a particular responsibility toward these victims of persecution and tyranny who are in our zone. We must make clear to the German people that we thoroughly abhor the Nazi policies of hatred and persecution. We have no better opportunity to demonstrate this than by the manner in which we ourselves actually treat the survivors remaining in Germany.

I hope you will report to me as soon as possible the steps you have been able to take to clean up the conditions mentioned in the report.

I am communicating directly with the British Government in an effort to have the doors of Palestine opened to such of these displaced persons as wish to go there.

Very sincerely yours,

Harry S. Truman

APPENDIX SEVEN

The President
The White House,
Washington.

My Dear Mr. President:

Pursuant to your letter of June 22, 1945, I have the honor to present to you a partial report upon my recent mission to Europe to inquire into (1) the conditions under which displaced persons and particularly those who may be stateless or non-repatriable are at present living, especially in Germany and Austria, (2) the needs of such persons, (3) how those needs are being met at present by the military authorities, the governments of residence and international and private relief bodies, and (4) the views of the possibly non-repatriable persons as to their future destinations.

My instructions were to give particular attention to the problems, needs and views of the Jewish refugees among the displaced people, especially in Germany and Austria. The report, particularly this partial report, accordingly deals in the main with that group.

On numerous occasions appreciation was expressed by the victims of Nazi persecution for the interest of the United States Government in them. As my report shows they are in need of attention and help. Up to this point they have been "liberated" more in a military sense than actually. For reasons explained in the report, their particular problems, to this time, have not been given attention to any appreciable extent; consequently, they feel that they, who were in so many ways the first and worst victims of nazism, are being neglected by their liberators.

Upon my request, the Department of State authorized Dr. Joseph J. Schwartz to join me in the mission. Dr. Schwartz, European Director of the American Joint Distribution Committee, was granted a leave of absence from that organization for the purpose of accompanying me. His long and varied experience in refugee problems, as well as his familiarity with the Continent and the people, made Dr. Schwartz a most valuable associate; this report represents our joint views, conclusions, and recommendations.

During various portions of the trip I had, also, the assistance of Mr. Patrick M. Malin, Vice-Director of the Intergovernmental Committee on Refugees and Mr. Herbert

Katzski of the War Refugee Board. These gentlemen, likewise, have had considerable experience in refugee matters. Their assistance and cooperation were most helpful in the course of the survey.

I. Germany and Austria: *Conditions*

(1) Generally speaking, three months after V-E Day and even longer after the liberation of individual groups, many Jewish displaced persons and other possibly non-repatriables are living under guard behind barbed-wire fences, in camps of several descriptions, (built by the Germans for slave-laborers and Jews) including some of the most notorious of the concentration camps, amidst crowded, frequently unsanitary and generally grim conditions, in complete idleness, with no opportunity, except surreptitiously, to communicate with the outside world, waiting, hoping for some word of encouragement and action in their behalf.

(2) While there has been marked improvement in the health of survivors of the Nazi starvation and persecution program, there are many pathetic malnutrition cases both among the hospitalized and in the general population of the camps. The death rate has been high since liberation, as was to be expected. One Army Chaplain, a Rabbi, personally attended, since liberation, 23,000 burials (90% Jews) at Bergen Belsen alone, one of the largest and most vicious of the concentration camps, where, incidentally, despite persistent reports to the contrary, fourteen thousand displaced persons are still living, including over seven thousand Jews. At many

of the camps and centers, including those where serious starvation cases are, there is a marked and serious lack of needed medical supplies.

(3) Although some Camp Commandants have managed, in spite of the many obvious difficulties, to find clothing of one kind or another for their charges, many of the Jewish displaced persons, late in July, had no clothing other than their concentration camp garb—a rather hideous striped pajama effect—while others, to their chagrin, were obliged to wear German S.S. uniforms. It is questionable which clothing they hate the more.

(4) With a few notable exceptions, nothing in the way of a program of activity or organized effort toward rehabilitation has been inaugurated and the internees, for they are literally such, have little to do except to dwell upon their plight, the uncertainty of their future and, what is more unfortunate, to draw comparisons between their treatment "under the Germans" and "in liberation." Beyond knowing that they are no longer in danger of the gas chambers, torture, and other forms of violent death, they see—and there is—little change. The morale of those who are either stateless or who do not wish to return to their countries of nationality is very low. They have witnessed great activity and efficiency in returning people to their homes but they hear or see nothing in the way of plans for them and consequently they wonder and frequently ask what "liberation" means. This situation is considerably accentuated where, as in so many cases, they are able to look from their crowded and bare quarters and see the German

civilian population, particularly in the rural areas, to all appearances living normal lives in their own homes.

(5) The most absorbing worry of these Nazi and war victims concerns relatives—wives, husbands, parents, children. Most of them have been separated for three, four, or five years and they cannot understand why the liberators should not have undertaken immediately the organized effort to re-unite family groups. Most of the very little which has been done in this direction has been informal action by the displaced persons themselves with the aid of devoted Army Chaplains, frequently Rabbis, and the American Joint Distribution Committee. Broadcasts of names and locations by the Psychological Warfare Division at Luxembourg have been helpful, although the lack of receiving sets has handicapped the effectiveness of the program. Even where, as has been happening, information has been received as to relatives living in other camps in Germany, it depends on the personal attitude and disposition of the Camp Commandant whether permission can be obtained or assistance received to follow up on the information. Some Camp Commandants are quite rigid in this particular, while others lend every effort to join family groups.

(6) It is difficult to evaluate the food situation fairly because one must be mindful of the fact that quite generally food is scarce and is likely to be more so during the winter ahead. On the other hand, in presenting the factual situation, one must raise the question as to how much longer many of these people, particularly those who have over such a long period felt persecution and near starvation, can survive on a

diet composed principally of bread and coffee, irrespective of the caloric content. In many camps, the 2,000 calories included 1,250 calories of a black, wet and extremely unappetizing bread. I received the distinct impression and considerable substantiating information that large numbers of the German population—again principally in the rural areas—have a more varied and palatable diet than is the case with the displaced persons. The Camp Commandants put in their requisitions with the German burgomeister and many seemed to accept whatever he turned over as being the best that was available.

(7) Many of the buildings in which displaced persons are housed are clearly unfit for winter use and everywhere there is great concern about the prospect of a complete lack of fuel. There is every likelihood that close to a million displaced persons will be in Germany and Austria when winter sets in. The outlook in many areas so far as shelter, food and fuel are concerned is anything but bright.

II. Needs of the Jews

While it is impossible to state accurately the number of Jews now in that part of Germany not under Russian occupation, all indications point to the fact that the number is small, with one hundred thousand probably the top figure; some informed persons contend the number is considerably smaller. The principal nationality groups are Poles, Hungarians, Rumanians, Germans and Austrians.

The first and plainest need of these people is a recognition of their actual status and by this I mean their status as Jews. Most of them have spent years in the worst of the concentration camps. In many cases, although the full extent is not yet known, they are the sole survivors of their families and many have been through the agony of witnessing the destruction of their loved ones. Understandably, therefore, their present condition, physical and mental, is far worse than that of other groups.

While SHAEF (now combined Displaced Persons Executive) policy directives have recognized formerly persecuted persons, including enemy and ex-enemy nationals, as one of the special categories of displaced persons, the general practice thus far has been to follow only nationality lines. While admittedly it is not normally desirable to set aside particular racial or religious groups from their nationality categories, the plain truth is that this was done for so long by the Nazis that a group has been created which has special needs. Jews as Jews (not as members of their nationality groups) have been more severely victimized than the non-Jewish members of the same or other nationalities.

When they are now considered only as members of nationality groups, the result is that special attention cannot be given to their admittedly greater needs because, it is contended, doing so would constitute preferential treatment and lead to trouble with the non-Jewish portion of the particular nationality group.

Thus there is a distinctly unrealistic approach to the problem. Refusal to recognize the Jews as such has the effect, in this situation, of closing one's eyes to their former and more barbaric persecution, which has already made them a separate group with greater needs.

Their second great need can be presented only by discussing what I found to be their

Wishes as to Future Destinations

(1) For reasons that are obvious and need not be labored, most Jews want to leave Germany and Austria as soon as possible. That is their first and great expressed wish and while this report necessarily deals with other needs present in the situation, many of the people themselves fear other suggestions or plans for their benefit because of the possibility that attention might thereby be diverted from the all-important matter of evacuation from Germany. Their desire to leave Germany is an urgent one. The life which they have led for the past ten years, a life of fear and wandering and physical torture, has made them impatient of delay. They want to be evacuated to Palestine now, just as other national groups are being repatriated to their homes. They do not look kindly on the idea of waiting around in idleness and in discomfort in a German camp for many months until a leisurely solution is found for them.

(2) Some wish to return to their countries of nationality but as to this there is considerable nationality variation. Very few Polish or Baltic Jews wish to return to their countries; higher percentages of the Hungarian and Rumanian groups want to return although some hasten to add that it may be only

temporarily in order to look for relatives. Some of the German Jews, especially those who have intermarried, prefer to stay in Germany.

(3) With respect to possible places of resettlement for those who may be stateless or who do not wish to return to their homes, Palestine is definitely and pre-eminently the first choice. Many now have relatives there, while others, having experienced intolerance and persecution in their homelands for years, feel that only in Palestine will they be welcomed and find peace and quiet and be given an opportunity to live and work. In the case of the Polish and the Baltic Jews, the desire to go to Palestine is based in a great majority of the cases on a love for the country and devotion to the Zionist ideal. It is also true, however, that there are many who wish to go to Palestine because they realize that their opportunity to be admitted into the United States or into other countries in the Western hemisphere is limited, if not impossible. Whatever the motive which causes them to turn to Palestine, it is undoubtedly true that the great majority of the Jews now in Germany do not wish to return to those countries from which they came.

(4) Palestine, while clearly the choice of most, is not the only named place of possible emigration. Some, but the number is not large, wish to emigrate to the United States where they have relatives, others to England, the British Dominions, or to South America.

Thus the second great need is the prompt development of

a plan to get out of Germany and Austria as many as possible of those who wish it.

Otherwise the needs and wishes of the Jewish groups among the displaced persons can be simply stated: among their physical needs are clothing and shoes (most sorely needed), more varied and palatable diet, medicines, beds and mattresses, reading materials. The clothing for the camps too is requisitioned from the German population, and whether there is not sufficient quantity to be had or the German population has not been willing or has not been compelled to give up sufficient quantity, the internees feel particularly bitter about the state of their clothing when they see how well the German population is still dressed. The German population today is still the best dressed population in all of Europe.

III. Manner in Which Needs Are Being Met

Aside from having brought relief from the fear of extermination, hospitalization for the serious starvation cases and some general improvement in conditions under which the remaining displaced persons are compelled to live, relatively little beyond the planning stage has been done, during the period of mass repatriation, to meet the special needs of the formerly persecuted groups.

UNRRA, being neither sufficiently organized or equipped nor authorized to operate displaced persons camps or centers on any large scale, has not been in position to make any substantial contribution to the situation. Regrettably there has been a disinclination on the part of many Camp Commandants to utilize UNRRA personnel even to the extent available, though it must be admitted that in many situations this resulted from unfortunate experiences Army officers had with UNRRA personnel who were unqualified and inadequate for the responsibility involved. Then, too, in the American and British zones, it too frequently occurred that UNRRA personnel did not include English-speaking members and this hampered proper working relationships.

Under these circumstances, UNRRA, to which has been assigned the responsibility for co-ordinating activities of private social welfare agencies, has been in awkward position when it came to considering and acting upon proposals of one kind or another submitted by well qualified agencies which would aid and supplement military and UNRRA responsibilities. The result has been that, up to this point, very few private social agencies are working with displaced persons, including the Jews, although the situation cries out for their services in many different ways.

It must be said, too, that because of their pre-occupation with mass repatriation and because of housing, personnel and transport difficulties, the military authorities have shown considerable resistance to the entrance of voluntary agency representatives, no matter how qualified they might be to help meet existing needs of displaced persons.

IV. Conclusions and Recommendations

1. Now that the worst of the pressure of mass repatriation is over, it is not unreasonable to suggest that in the next and perhaps more difficult period those who have suffered most and longest be given first and not last attention.

Specifically, in the days immediately ahead, the Jews in Germany and Austria should have the first claim upon the conscience of the people of the United States and Great Britain and the military and other personnel who represent them in work being done in Germany and Austria.

2. Evacuation from Germany should be the emphasized theme, policy and practice.

(a) Recognizing that repatriation is most desirable from the standpoint of all concerned, the Jews who wish to return to their own countries should be aided to do so without further delay. Whatever special action is needed to accomplish this with respect to countries of reception or consent of military or other authorities should be undertaken with energy and determination. Unless this and other action, about to be suggested, is taken, substantial unofficial and unauthorized movements of people must be expected, and these will require considerable force to prevent, for the patience of many of the persons involved is, and in my opinion with justification, nearing the breaking point. It cannot be overemphasized that many of these people are now desperate, that they have become accustomed under German rule to employ every possible means to reach their end, and that the fear of death does not restrain them.

(b) With respect to those who do not, for good reason, wish to return to their homes, prompt planning should likewise be undertaken. In this connection, the issue of Palestine must be faced. Now that such large numbers are no longer involved and if there is any genuine sympathy for what these survivors have endured, some reasonable extension or modification of the British White Paper of 1939 ought to be possible without too serious repercussions. For some of the European Jews, there is no acceptable or even decent solution for their future other than Palestine. This is said on a purely humanitarian basis with no reference to ideological or political considerations so far as Palestine is concerned.

It is my understanding, based upon reliable information, that certificates for immigration to Palestine will be practically exhausted by the end of the current month (August 1945). What is the future to be? To anyone who has visited the concentration camps and who has talked with the despairing survivors, it is nothing short of calamitous to contemplate that the gates of Palestine should be soon closed.

The Jewish Agency of Palestine has submitted to the British Government a petition that one hundred thousand additional immigration certificates be made available. A memorandum accompanying the petition makes a persuasive showing with respect to the immediate absorptive capacity of Palestine and the current, actual man-power shortages there.

While there may be room for difference of opinion as to the precise number of such certificates which might under the circumstances be considered reasonable, there is no question but that the request thus made would, if granted, contribute much to the sound solution for the future of Jews still in Germany and Austria and even other displaced Jews, who do not wish either to remain there or to return to their countries of nationality.

No other single matter is, therefore, so important from the viewpoint of Jews in Germany and Austria and those elsewhere who have known the horrors of the concentration camps as is the disposition of the Palestine question.

Dr. Hugh Dalton, a prominent member of the new British Government, is reported as having said at the Labour Party Conference in May 1945:

"This Party has laid it down and repeated it so recently as last April . . . that this time, having regard to the unspeakable horrors that have been perpetrated upon the Jews of Germany and other occupied countries in Europe, it is morally wrong and politically indefensible to impose obstacles to the entry into Palestine now of any Jews who desire to go there . . . .

"We also have stated clearly that this is not a matter which should be regarded as one for which the British Government alone should take responsibility; but as it comes, as do many others, in the international field, it is indispensable that there should be close agreement and cooperation among the British, American, and Soviet Governments, particularly if we are going to get a sure settlement in Palestine and the surrounding countries ...."

If this can be said to represent the viewpoint of the new Government in Great Britain, it certainly would not be inappropriate for the United States Government to express its interest in and support of some equitable solution of the question which would make it possible for some reasonable number of Europe's persecuted Jews, now homeless under any fair view, to resettle in Palestine. That is their wish and it is rendered desirable by the generally-accepted policy of permitting family groups to unite or reunite.

(c) The United States should, under existing immigration laws, permit reasonable numbers of such persons to come here, again particularly those who have family ties in this country. As indicated earlier, the number who desire emigration to the United States is not large.

If Great Britain and the United States were to take the actions recited, it might the more readily be that other countries would likewise be willing to keep their doors reasonably open for such humanitarian considerations and to demonstrate in a practical manner their disapproval of Nazi policy which unfortunately has poisoned so much of Europe.

3. To the extent that such emigration from Germany and Austria is delayed, some immediate temporary solution must be found. In any event there will be a substantial number of the

persecuted persons who are not physically fit or otherwise presently prepared for emigration.

Here I feel strongly that greater and more extensive efforts should be made to get them out of camps for they are sick of living in camps. In the first place, there is real need for such specialized places as (a) tuberculosis sanitaria and (b) rest homes for those who are mentally ill or who need a period of readjustment before living again in the world at large—anywhere. Some will require at least short periods of training or retraining before they can be really useful citizens.

But speaking more broadly, there is an opportunity here to give some real meaning to the policy agreed upon at Potsdam. If it be true, as seems to be widely conceded, that the German people at large do not have any sense of guilt with respect to the war and its causes and results, and if the policy is to be "To convince the German people that they have suffered a total military defeat and that they cannot escape responsibility for what they have brought upon themselves," then it is difficult to understand why so many displaced persons, particularly those who have so long been persecuted and whose repatriation or resettlement is likely to be delayed, should be compelled to live in crude, over-crowded camps while the German people, in rural areas, continue undisturbed in their homes.

As matters now stand, we appear to be treating the Jews as the Nazis treated them except that we do not exterminate them. They are in concentration camps in large numbers under our military guard instead of S.S. troops. One is led to wonder whether the German people, seeing this, are not supposing that we are following or at least condoning Nazi policy.

It seems much more equitable and as it should be to witness the very few places where fearless and uncompromising military officers have either requisitioned an entire village for the benefit of displaced persons, compelling the German population to find housing where they can, or have required the local population to billet a reasonable number of them. Thus the displaced persons, including the persecuted, live more like normal people and less like prisoners or criminals or herded sheep. They are in Germany, most of them and certainly the Jews, through no fault or wish of their own. This fact is in this fashion being brought home to the German people but it is being done on too small a scale.

At many places, however, the military government officers manifest the utmost reluctance or indisposition, if not timidity, about inconveniencing the German population. They even say that their job is to get communities working properly and soundly again, that they must "live with the Germans while the DPs (displaced persons) are a more temporary problem." Thus (and I am ready to cite the example) if a group of Jews are ordered to vacate their temporary quarters, needed for military purposes, and there are two possible sites, one a block of flats (modest apartments) with conveniences and the other a series of shabby buildings with outside toilet and washing facilities, the burgomeister readily succeeds in persuading the Town

Major to allot the latter to the displaced persons and to save the former for returning German civilians.

This tendency reflects itself in other ways, namely, in the employment of German civilians in the offices of military government officers when equally qualified personnel could easily be found among the displaced persons whose repatriation is not imminent. Actually there have been situations where displaced persons, especially Jews, have found it difficult to obtain audiences with military government authorities because ironically they have been obliged to go through German employees who have not facilitated matters.

Quite generally, insufficient use is made of the services of displaced persons. Many of them are able and eager to work but apparently they are not considered in this regard. While appreciating that language difficulties are sometimes involved, I am convinced that, both within and outside camps, greater use could be made of the personal services of those displaced persons who in all likelihood will be on hand for some time. Happily in some camps every effort is made to utilize the services of the displaced persons and these are apt to be the best camps in all respects.

4. To the extent that (a) evacuation from Germany and Austria is not immediately possible and (b) the formerly persecuted groups cannot be housed in villages or billeted with the German population, I recommend urgently that separate camps be set up for Jews or at least for those who

wish, in the absence of a better solution, to be in such camps. There are several reasons for this: (1) a great majority want it; (2) it is the only way in which administratively their special needs and problems can be met without charges of preferential treatment or (oddly enough) charges of "discrimination" with respect to Jewish agencies now prepared and ready to give them assistance.

In this connection, I wish to emphasize that it is not a case of singling out a particular group for special privileges. It is a matter of raising to a more normal level the position of a group which has been depressed to the lowest depths conceivable by years of organized and inhuman oppression. The measures necessary for their restitution do not come within any reasonable interpretation of privileged treatment and are required by considerations of justice and humanity.

There has been some tendency at spots in the direction of separate camps for those who might be found to be stateless or non-repatriable or whose repatriation is likely to be deferred some time. Actually, too, this was announced some time ago as SHAEF policy but in practice it has not been taken to mean much for there is (understandably if not carried too far) a refusal to contemplate possible statelessness and an insistence, in the interests of the large repatriation program, to consider all as repatriable. This results in a resistance to anything in the way of special planning for the "hard core," although all admit it is there and will inevitably appear. While speaking of camps, this should be pointed out: While it may be that conditions in Germany and Austria are still such that certain control measures are required, there seems little justification for the continuance of barbed-wire fences, armed guards, and prohibition against leaving the camp except by passes, which at some places are illiberally granted. Prevention of looting is given as the reason for these stern measures but it is interesting that in portions of the Seventh Army area where greater liberty of movement in and out of camps is given there is actually much less plundering than in other areas where people, wishing to leave camp temporarily, must do so by stealth.

5. As quickly as possible, the actual operation of the camps should be turned over to a civilian agency—UNRRA. That organization is aware of weaknesses in its present structure and is pressing to remedy them. In that connection, it is believed that greater assistance could be given by the military authorities, upon whom any civilian agency in Germany and Austria today is necessarily dependent so far as housing, transport, and other items are concerned. While it is true the military have been urging UNRRA to get ready to assume responsibility, it is also the fact that insufficient cooperation of an active nature has been given to accomplish the desired end.

6. Since, in any event, the military authorities must necessarily continue to participate in the program for all displaced persons, especially with respect to housing, transport, security, and certain supplies, it is recommended that there be a review of the military personnel selected for Camp Commandant positions. Some serving at present, while perhaps adequate for the mass repatriation job, are manifestly unsuited for the longer-term job of working in a camp composed of

people whose repatriation or resettlement is likely to be delayed. Officers who have had some background or experience in social welfare work are to be preferred and it is believed there are some who are available. It is most important that the officers selected be sympathetic with the program and that they be temperamentally able to work and to cooperate with UNRRA and other relief and welfare agencies.

7. Pending the assumption of responsibility for operations by UNRRA, it would be desirable if a more extensive plan of field visitation by appropriate Army Group Headquarters be instituted. It is believed that many of the conditions now existing in the camps would not be tolerated if more intimately known by supervisory officers through inspection tours.

8. It is urgently recommended that plans for tracing services, now under consideration, be accelerated to the fullest extent possible and that, in this same direction, communication services, if on open postal cards only, be made available to displaced persons within Germany and Austria as soon as possible. The difficulties are appreciated but it is believed that if the anxiety of the people, so long abused and harassed, were fully understood, ways and means could be found within the near future to make such communication and tracing of relatives possible. I believe also that some of the private agencies could be helpful in this direction if given an opportunity to function.

V. Other Comments

While I was instructed to report conditions as I found them, the following should be added to make the picture complete:

(1) A gigantic task confronted the occupying armies in Germany and Austria in getting back to their homes as many as possible of the more than six million displaced persons found in those countries. Less than three months after V-E Day, more than four million of such persons have been repatriated—a phenomenal performance. One's first impression, in surveying the situation, is that of complete admiration for what has been accomplished by the military authorities in so materially reducing the time as predicted to be required for this stupendous task. Praise of the highest order is due all military units with respect to this phase of the post-fighting job. In directing attention to existing conditions which unquestionably required remedying, there is no intention or wish to detract one particle from the preceding statements.

(2) While I did not actually see conditions as they existed immediately after liberation, I had them described in detail sufficient to make entirely clear that there has been, during the intervening period, some improvement in the conditions under which most of the remaining displaced persons are living. Reports which have come out of Germany informally from refugees themselves and from persons interested in refugee groups indicate something of a tendency not to take into account the full scope of the overwhelming task and re-

sponsibilities facing the military authorities. While it is understandable that those who have been persecuted and otherwise mistreated over such a long period should be impatient at what appears to them to be undue delay in meeting their special needs, fairness dictates that, in evaluating the progress made, the entire problem and all of its ramifications be kept in mind. My effort has been, therefore, to weigh quite carefully the many complaints made to me in the course of my survey, both by displaced persons themselves and in their behalf, in the light of the many responsibilities which confronted the military authorities.

(3) While for the sake of brevity this report necessarily consisted largely of general statements, it should be recognized that exceptions exist with respect to practically all of such generalizations. One high ranking military authority predicted, in advance of my trip through Germany and Austria, that I would find, with respect to camps containing displaced persons, "some that are quite good, some that are very bad, with the average something under satisfactory." My subsequent trip confirmed that prediction in all respects.

In order to file this report promptly so that possibly some remedial steps might be considered at as early a date as possible, I have not taken time to analyze all of the notes made in the course of the trip or to comment on the situation in France, Belgium, Holland, or Switzerland, also visited. Accordingly, I respectfully request that this report be considered as partial in nature. The problems present in Germany and Austria are much more serious and difficult than in any of the other countries named and this fact, too, seemed to make desirable the filing of a partial report immediately upon completion of the mission.

In conclusion, I wish to repeat that the main solution, in many ways the only real solution, of the problem lies in the quick evacuation of all non-repatriable Jews in Germany and Austria, who wish it, to Palestine. In order to be effective, this plan must not be long delayed. The urgency of the situation should be recognized. It is inhuman to ask people to continue to live for any length of time under their present conditions. The evacuation of the Jews of Germany and Austria to Palestine will solve the problem of the individuals involved and will also remove a problem from the military authorities who have had to deal with it. The army's ability to move millions of people quickly and efficiently has been amply demonstrated. The evacuation of a relatively small number of Jews from Germany and Austria will present no great problem to the military. With the end of the Japanese war, the shipping situation should also become sufficiently improved to make such a move feasible. The civilized world owes it to this handful of survivors to provide them with a home where they can again settle down and begin to live as human beings.

Respectfully,

Earl G. Harrison

Hutler, Albert A.
Agony of silence.

DATE DUE

AP 05 '91			
NO 15 '91			
JA 28 '94			